Backpack Like You Mean It

A crackpot tale of travel through Southeast Asia

Jennifer A. Neves

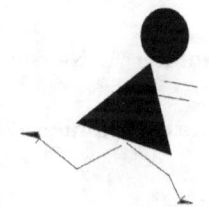

Mad Dash Publishing

Backpack Like You Mean It
A crackpot tale of travel through Southeast Asia

Mad Dash Publishing

All rights reserved. No part of this book may be reproduced or transmitted in any form or by any means, electronic or mechanical, including photocopying, recording or by any information storage and retrieval system, without written permission from the author, except for the inclusion of brief quotations in a review.

Copyright © 2012 by Jennifer A. Neves

Library of Congress Control Number: 2012900922

ISBN 978-0-9850476-0-3
Kindle ISBN 978-0-9850476-1-0
ePub ISBN 978-0-9850476-2-7

Cover art and illustrations copyright © 2012 by Sarah-Lee Terrat

Printed in the United States of America

Backpack Like You Mean It

Preface – Note To The Reader

The information regarding monkeys within this book has no factual basis. The author suffers from an irrational fear of having her face ripped off.

Backpack Like You Mean It

ACKNOWLEDGEMENTS

I would like to thank my parents, *Anthony* and *Helene Neves* for encouraging me to take risks, live boldly and create my own opportunities. A special thanks also goes to *Alan Boright*, *Don Schultz*, *Kristin Peet*, and *Sandy Shenk* for taking the time to read and edit my manuscript. Your suggestions and encouragement were invaluable. I am also indebted to *Heather Cole* for her unconditional support and brutal honesty in matters of writing and life.

Most important, I would like to thank *Nathan*. He is my muse, my travel companion, and my best friend.

Warning – Disclaimer

This book was written to provide entertainment. It is not meant as a travel guide, or a definitive resource on anything, especially traveling through Southeast Asia. It is sold with the understanding that the publisher and author are not engaged in rendering legal, travel, or any other professional advice.

This text should not be used in preparing for or executing international travel. The information herein is unreliable at best and suffers from artistic embellishment. All names have been changed to protect the innocent, ignorant, and incorrigible. The purpose of this book is to entertain. The author and Mad Dash Publishing shall have neither liability nor responsibility to any person or entity with respect to any loss or damage caused, or alleged to have been caused, directly or indirectly, by the information contained in this book. If one does not wish to be bound by the above, they may give this book to someone else.

Karmaseatra

Chapter One

Thailand
Headfirst in the Shallow End

I am a plane sleeper. It doesn't matter how small, how loud, how many babies are crying or filling their diapers, I sleep. I channel my inner contortionist, find a place to lay or dangle my head, and slip into unconsciousness. There are consequences. Often, I wake with one or several of my body parts invading others' personal space. Sometimes I wake to discover I am suffering from complete paralysis due to poor circulation. The worst is when I am both paralyzed and resting my hand awkwardly on the thigh of an elderly woman.

Maybe it was a blessing that this plane ride was different. My eyes were wide with anticipation, and my brain was abuzz. I had the caffeine shakes without the caffeine. I was sitting next to Nathan, my best friend in the world, on a one-way ticket to Southeast Asia. I had arranged a single night's stay at a hostel in Bangkok, but nothing else. My uncharacteristically disorganized departure from the United States had me on edge. I was a little annoyed by Nathan's calm. He was asleep beside me, drooling slightly, and snoring. He had fallen asleep almost immediately after boarding.

The last month had been a whirlwind for us both. We had dropped everything to make the trip possible. We left our jobs, our apartments, and said goodbye to our friends and family. In the spirit of embracing massive lifestyle changes, we also chose to timidly test the waters of our relationship. I don't know why we thought that taking our three-year friendship to another level, right before being trapped in a foreign country together, was a good idea. It's probably on the top-ten list of things *not* to do before traveling with someone. Our friends cringed at the news. One even gave her condolences. Nathan's mother gave a bit of advice, perhaps inspired by her own concern. She told him to make big changes slowly. Make them one at a time, with caution.

I also received advice from my parents. My father's advice was more inspired by movies featuring overseas abductions than anything else. He put a hand gently on my shoulder and said, "Be safe. Have fun. And remember Jenny, I was killed in a tragic farming accident. There is no money for ransom if you are kidnapped."

My mother's advice was even less helpful. "Don't talk to strangers."

I was struck by a pang of anxiety, a vague sense that I had forgotten something important, when my eyes focused on the tiny T.V. screen on the seat-back in front of me. There were words on the screen, but I couldn't read them. My stomach tightened when it came to me. The Thai language wasn't written with English letters, so the little piece of paper that I had in my bag, with the English address of our hostel in Bangkok, would be of no use. Carrying around the translations of Thai street signs was foolish. How had I not realized that knowing our hostel was on *Kings Road* would do me absolutely no good? The word *King*, written in Thai, was a series of beautifully artistic squiggles.

Looking over at Nathan, I wondered if I should mention how unprepared we were for our arrival. He looked so peaceful sleeping beside me. I decided to let him rest; we would have plenty of time later to worry about being stranded on the dark streets of Bangkok. I was certain Nathan wouldn't hold my mistake against me, considering his own distaste for planning. He wasn't the type to over prepare. In most cases, he made no effort to prepare at all. I had accepted this character blemish long ago, tossing it into the list of reasons I found him charming.

As a perfect example, he had started packing and selling his belongings two days before he was scheduled to be homeless. I, on the other hand, was the extreme opposite. I had spent the last six months living below the poverty line to save cash. I gave five months' notice at work and started the process of packing and selling my belongings far too soon. It was hard to fight the urge. I put most of my furniture and appliances on craigslist. The toaster was one of the first things to go. I didn't realize how much I used the toaster until it was gone. Then the living room chairs went, then the table, then the lamps. It wasn't until one Friday night, almost a month before I needed to move, that I realized I had seriously disrupted my quality of life. I was sitting on the living room floor wearing a headlamp, trying to enjoy a peanut butter toast that I had cooked on an electric stove top, which was smoking, because if you put bread on electric coils, it sticks. The smoke detector wailed tauntingly as if to point out, "I'm not yours to sell, nitwit."

I had been so excited to drop everything and travel. I still was, but the reality of it was just starting to settle in. I needed a distraction to calm my nerves. The airline won my undying affection with a tutorial on Thai numbers. I stared attentively at the tiny screen in front of me. It took the better part of an hour to learn the correct pronunciation for the numbers one through ten. Most were fairly easy, but from my lips, the number eight sounded like the cry of an injured animal. I accidentally woke Nathan with my braying. When he realized what I was doing, he started up his own tutorial.

While he worked, I checked to make sure all of our documents were in order: our hostel reservation number, passports, customs paperwork, and our newly acquired fraudulent return tickets. I had arrived and checked in at JFK airport a bit before Nathan and was informed that if I wanted to be permitted into Thailand, I was going to need a return or continuing ticket. The ticket would prove that I wasn't planning to outstay my welcome (thirty days for Americans). Fortunately, my distress at hearing this inspired sympathy in my airline representative. Just this once he was going to do me a favor. Wink. He was going to have his friend in ticketing print off a fake booking for a return flight at the end of February. Wink, wink. I managed to get Nathan's name on the document as well.

With fake tickets in hand, I went searching for Nathan. I spotted him chatting with his parents across the expansive ticketing hall. His blue eyes were wide with excitement as he explained some last-minute detail to his father. I couldn't help but smile at how much he naturally fit the stereotype of a backpacker. His unruly blond hair stuck out in every direction, and his red beard was tangled and thick. It had grown since the last time I had seen him. His lean frame shouldered a small pack that I hoped was his carry-on, though I wouldn't have put it past him to leave for a six-month journey with so little.

I had never met his parents and was a bit nervous about doing so. My friend Heather, who had accompanied me to the airport, dutifully whispered encouraging words as we neared them. She was carrying one of my bags and looked just as excited as I'm sure I looked. Nathan's parents appeared confused. Their eyes darted from me to Heather and back to me again. They weren't sure which of us was the one running away with their son. I doubted that Nathan had given them the slightest hint about my appearance. Heather and I both had brown hair, though mine was short, curly, and unruly where hers was tied back in a long ponytail. I decided that as a backpacker, I could get away with ignoring my thick, frizzy hair. Nathan assured me that it looked fantastic even in high humidity, but I suspected it often resembled a matted raccoon pelt.

When Heather and I were within earshot, I thought to reveal our identities by shouting, "Hi, I'm the one taking your son to a foreign country to ruin his career and steal his innocence," but resisted the urge. Heather was wearing a vest covered in what looked to be human hair and had glitter stuck in the wrinkly skin of her ears and eyelids. There was also a grain of rice stuck in her eyebrow, which I admit, I should have mentioned to her, but it made me smile every time I saw it. Plus, rice was fitting for a Southeast Asian send-off.

While I politely shook hands with Nathan's parents, he picked the rice out of Heather's eyebrow and handed it to her. She looked over at me, rolled her eyes, and gave me a hug before disappearing into the crowd. When I gave Nathan his fake booking, I was surprised to learn that his airline representative hadn't mentioned a thing to him. She was probably hoping to see him again in a week, post-deportation. She may have also assumed he wouldn't need a return ticket because he wasn't going to make it through security. Unfortunately for Nathan, something about his appearance gives strangers worldwide the impression that he's on drugs. An impression which is entirely inaccurate. His brain shuts down with medications as innocuous as throat lozenges.

After saying goodbye to his parents, we turned and made our way to an escalator. I could feel their eyes on us as we rode slowly toward the departure gates. We must have looked like quite the pair from behind; proof that opposites attract. Nathan stands six feet tall, and I just over five feet. Our complexions are on opposite ends of the spectrum. His skin is fair and highly susceptible to sunburns, while my Portuguese ancestry provides me with brown eyes and skin for protection against the elements.

Some of our differences were extremely practical in terms of being traveling partners. Our height difference made the division of labor between the two of us a no-brainer. Nathan handled all of our business located four feet or higher from the ground. I handled things like sweeping, picking things up off of the floor, and anything happening in sinks. I realize this list of responsibilities might sound sexist, but for someone with the compulsion to make beds, organize everything, and an obsessive attention to meaningless detail, my responsibilities suited me perfectly.

Nathan was assigned another critically important chore, which I felt evened the playing fields. He was responsible for all navigation. It was clear at the start of the journey that I would have no official role in finding *anything*. I would not be responsible for reading maps but storing and maintaining them fell within my jurisdiction.

My thoughts were interrupted by the sound of Nathan's hand crashing into my meal tray. When he had finished with his

Thai numbers, he had found another tutorial in the seat-back library. It was an exercise video for passengers, meant to improve circulation and emotional health. His arms and legs were flailing aggressively in all directions. While he did the seated version of a yoga sun salutation, I did my best to appear unattached to the crazy person beside me. But I *was* attached to him. We were going to be inseparable for the next six months.

It was hard to believe that merely three weeks earlier I had shown up on his doorstep, having quit my job and sold all of my things, to help him do the same. I had arrived on New Year's Eve. He had warned me that there were still a few loose ends to tie up before we took leave of our friends and family, but I had been unaware of how drastically different his definition of *a few* was from my own. He had done remarkably little, if anything, to clean, pack, and prepare for the journey. He still had to get out of his apartment, quit his job, and sell most of his things. These tasks apparently did not excite him as they had me. He had put them all off until the absolute last minute, then slightly beyond. When he opened his apartment door for me, early on the morning of December 31st, things looked like they always did, which concerned me greatly. He was expected to have the apartment cleaned and empty by the early morning of January 1st, at which time the new tenants were planning to move in. We had one day to pack up his life and fit it into a Mazda hatchback.

We drank our coffee quickly and began to work. From seven in the morning until half-past eleven that night, I scrubbed floors, walls, and dishes. I saw a side of Nathan that I wish I hadn't seen. I discovered petrified cat vomit under his bed. I discovered petrified cat vomit in some of his shoes, in closets, and hardened on the outside of his sleeping bag. He explained that his ex-cat, Gus, had been sent away to live with his parents, for psychological reasons. It too had been petrified: to be alone, to be petted for too long, or not long enough, to be talked to in a loud voice, or a whisper. It hadn't liked strangers, or people who smelled friendly, or the sound of laughter; the list was endless. I question whether these dislikes might not have been boiled down to a single dislike: Nathan. This poor bulimic cat puked on everything it could get its face near, trying to send the message. Unfortunately for Gus and me, Nathan hadn't even noticed the vomit all over his apartment.

 Once I had finished with cat bile cleanup, I started scrubbing Nathan's refrigerator. While I dislodged a green bean from the door's rubber seal, he mentioned that his travel fund had just been sucker punched by the natural gas company. He had received a gas bill for the last seven months of his time on Adams Street. At first, he thought it was a mistake. A gas bill for almost a thousand dollars didn't seem possible. However, the company explained to him in excruciating detail that his apartment was the only one in the building with natural gas heating. The door that never closed into the hallway and the vents from his living room into the upstairs neighbor's apartment had been heating the entire building all winter. This is the kind of surprise that devastates most people. However, Nathan has an incredible ability to roll with bad news. He shrugs his shoulders, utters a choice word, then moves past it.

 I admire that about him. Truly I do. I will openly admit, in this case, my first emotion wasn't admiration, but I was too excited about our upcoming adventure to let his dwindling bank account bother me. We finished the job with just enough time to pack his car, lock the doors, and head north to a New Year's Eve party that was about to reach its climax. We arrived at my brother's place with thirty seconds to spare. The clock struck midnight just as we were dropping our bags to the floor. The start of our adventure began with a kiss.

 My recollections were interrupted by a flavorless TV dinner and a warning from our flight attendant not to touch the oxygen bag that had just plopped down on top of Nathan's head. He was sleeping again, so I scribbled a note that read, *Do not touch the oxygen mask*, and placed it on his lap before slipping into my own restless sleep. The remainder of the flight was spent in a groggy haze. We were fed five different times; each meal tasted like boiled peas and soggy breaded meat sticks. When we finally arrived at the Bangkok International Airport, we were bloated and exhausted. It was the middle of the night, but the airport was teeming with travelers.

It took forty-five minutes to get to the immigration desk. While we waited, I read airport signage to ensure we met the requirements for entrance into the Kingdom of Thailand. Above the immigration desk were the following rules:

1. *Travelers must provide bank statement showing more than USD 1500.*
2. *Women must show respect by dressing conservatively when appropriate.*
3. *Travelers must possess a return or continuing ticket.*

I was slightly concerned by the list, considering our return ticket was fake, neither one of us could prove we weren't poor, and my tank top had spaghetti straps. My worry was needless. Coming from the United States, one expects customs officials to be experts in turning innocent questions to ferocious accusations. In the U.S., the question, "You are here as a tourist?" sounds like, "You are here as a God damned terrorist aren't you?" In Thailand, it's more like, "You are a beautiful Goddess, please stay and enjoy yourself." In Southeast Asia, customs officials are more like customer service specialists than law enforcement officials. They are more concerned about making good first impressions than deterring criminals.

*

Before continuing with our experiences in Thailand, I feel the need to confess that I considered not writing about Thailand at all. It was our first stop on a six-month adventure. We were new to backpacking, and just as in any new undertaking, we were inexperienced and sloppy. Nathan and I needed time to become decent travelers, to notice things that mattered instead of being overwhelmed by every experience. We were consumed by the silly details, like toilet paper scarcity, instead of the important ones, like toilet scarcity. We only just scratched the surface in the art of sincerely connecting to local people.

As it turned out, Thailand was the perfect country for introducing ourselves to the traveling mentality. It had an impenetrable tourist-friendly facade. A nation that tourism largely supported, its citizens are taught from a young age that money comes with happy customers. Locals are uneasy about showing emotions beyond pleasure and hospitality. New to the travel business, we were probably incapable of handling anything less. We were, for the most part, easily frustrated, confused, and cautious. Babies with backpacks.

Hostel Environment

It took us almost three hours to find our way from the airport to the hostel I had booked online. The easy part was finding a train into the city. We rode it to the end of the line and were relieved to find a stack of free maps, in English, just outside of the station. Nathan stood looking down at one, troubled.

"Well, it's nice to have a map in English. I can see that our hostel is way over here, on this street," he said, pointing at a spot at the outer limits of the page. "But, none of the road signs are in English, so I don't know where we are. Also, it's cloudy, so we need to find a landmark to determine north from south."

I tried to sound casual, "Yeah, I meant to mention it to you earlier…that it might be difficult to find our hostel."

Nathan's head shot up, "How much earlier?"

"I realized on the plane, when we were learning our Thai numbers, that we were in a bit of a pickle." I tried to lighten the mood with a smile, then jovially punched Nathan on the shoulder, "It's an adventure!"

We both went back to staring at the map intently. The dim yellow light above our heads began to flicker. Car horns and police sirens wailed somewhere in the distance. I suddenly became aware of how unnaturally still everything was, and how dreadful it smelled. How had we ended up in such squalid desolation? Where were the people? It felt as though we were on the verge of being murdered by a knife-wielding drug addict. We were standing under an overpass, wearing gigantic hiking packs, studying a tiny piece of paper. We couldn't possibly have advertised any more clearly that we were vulnerable.

Movement caught my eye.

From the shadows, a young man wearing dark clothes emerged. He was the only person we had seen since getting off the train. He must have sensed our wariness, because he stopped several paces away and asked if we needed help. As outsiders, we didn't know if he was a mugger, or a good Samaritan. We took our chances, pointed to where we wanted to go on our map, and asked which direction it was. He told us, but hesitantly. Then he added, "You don't want to go there. There's nothing out there."

We didn't have a plan B. We thanked the stranger, then started off in the direction of our hostel. I kept a close eye on him until he disappeared down a side street, wondering if he might be circling around behind us for an attack. Nathan interrupted my paranoia with a revelation. "The one thing that tourist maps of cities worldwide are notorious for missing, is scale. We know where our hostel is on the map, and now we know where we are, but we could be half a mile from our destination or ten miles."

"I'm sure it's much closer to half a mile." I was trying to convince myself, as much as Nathan. "The street our hostel is on looks so close to the little dot that marked the train station. A quick jaunt. An evening stroll. We'll be there in no time."

It was nearly midnight; the streets were empty, and the windows of businesses and homes were dark. The farther we walked, the more isolated and barren things became. It felt wrong, like we were walking away from the city. There was nothing else to do but keep walking. No taxis passed us, no busses. We couldn't read signs at street corners or hanging from overpasses. Nathan began to grasp at straws. We had seen Thai letters in the airport, so he started comparing the letters we saw on signs to the letters we had seen elsewhere. "You see that one? That one looks like the head of a bird with its beak pointing up. I saw that letter on the train station map."

It seemed like a pointless exercise to me, but I think it gave him hope that he could reason his way to our hostel. Little did I know that his interest in deciphering the Thai language would become a full-blown obsession. From that moment, he became unfailingly committed to the task.

I felt responsible for our predicament. I had been the one to book our lodging online. I had already undermined my credibility when it came to picking hostels on the Internet. The night before, we'd had a one-night layover in a room that I also booked, in Hong Kong; it had been about as safe and clean as a dumpster. We trudged on. After about forty minutes of walking, still in relatively good spirits because our adventure had finally begun, we passed a group of soldiers with huge smiles. I waved happily as we walked past. When we were out of earshot, Nathan exclaimed, "Holy shit! Did you see the size of their guns?"

"Guns? No. They were all so friendly and had beautiful uniforms. I was distracted by their smiles."

"Seriously?" he asked.

I answered, "Did you notice how colorful their uniforms were?"

Nathan was shaking his head, "I missed their smiles *and* their outfits. I was distracted by their *huge* guns!"

In my defense, they were the friendliest soldiers I had ever laid eyes on.

Eventually, we found ourselves peering into a dark alley. Several seedy individuals were lingering in the shadows, watching us watch them. Nathan used his best slow-motion head turn to accentuate the dramatic eyebrow raise he had been saving for the last hour and a half, "Our hostel is down there?"

"Listen, I booked this thing online. The Internet can be misleading. It's around here somewhere."

Thankfully, we were gazing down the wrong alley. An older woman who picked up on our distress helped us find our hostel, which was located two alleys farther down the street. It had an elegant and professional sign, a clean common area, and a friendly receptionist. We settled in, then the owner took us out for a very late dinner and explained some of the basics of Thai living. The only thing I remembered from his extensive list of warnings was not to touch a monk. I was redeemed in Nathan's eyes. Our room was clean, and we had been treated to dinner like honored guests.

After our meal, I took the first shift in the shower. We had been on the move for almost two days and I had no intention of jumping into a clean bed, covered with grime. I left Nathan sitting patiently on the edge of the bed, waiting his turn. When I peeked my head out thirty-seconds later, to ask for help in turning the hot water on, he was dead asleep. I suffered through an icy shower, which erased all thought of rest from my mind. I spent the next hour washing our clothes by hand in the sink, though the pair of socks Nathan had pulled from his feet before collapsing could have easily washed themselves.

The Accidental Nap

We woke early the next morning, our first full day in Thailand, like zombies with hangovers. The jet lag had wreaked havoc on our internal clocks. Besides being tired, we also struggled with the excruciating temperature difference between New York and Bangkok. The minor exertion of unpacking clean clothes from my backpack caused beads of sweat to form all over my body. As Nathan unpacked, his face took on a look of genuine surprise. I was mesmerized by the way he was seemingly flustered by the contents of his own bag. Then, I realized he truly didn't recognize half of it. Not because it wasn't his, but because it wasn't what he had expected to find.

Nathan has a knack for getting himself into strange and entirely avoidable situations. He took the discovery of his backpack's contents with calm, quizzical acceptance. During the packing process, he had apparently grabbed several piles of items he did *not* want to take on the trip, which had been stacked neatly on his bed next to the piles of things he *did* want to take along. This left him in a hostel room in Bangkok with things like spoons and forks, three collared dress shirts, unnervingly few pairs of underwear, three pairs of sneakers, and no toiletries. Thankfully, one or two of the correct piles did make it into his bag. He had the camera, his iPod, and a couple of pairs of shorts.

After a quick breakfast, we stepped from the lobby of our hostel with smiles on our faces and wads of baht in our wallets. The room had been hot even with air conditioning, but the temperature in the city at nine in the morning was much worse; it was like walking into a greenhouse. I couldn't tell if the air was humid or if my skin was slippery because my sweat glands had exploded. For the first time, we were able to see the neighborhood we had walked so far to find the night before. My suspicion that we had been walking away from the city was confirmed. We could see the city in the distance, looming in the hazy skyline. We both knew that we weren't ready for it. We were too new, too naive to handle the dangers that lurked there. We decided instead to walk to the old quarter. It was apparently where most backpackers spent their time. We *were* backpackers, after all.

The streets were busy with taxis, mopeds, and tuk tuks. We knew of the tuk tuk but hadn't seen one yet. The tuk tuk is a Southeast Asian taxi. It is smaller than a car, but larger than a moped, so able to carry more passengers. Some looked like ATVs with one of the front wheels missing; some were jury-rigged motorized bicycles. All had a two- to four-person carriage swinging erratically behind, and all were driven by a man who took great pride in his ability to move speedily through the most harrowing traffic situations. No matter the design, they were all driven by lunatics.

We crossed a busy street, enduring the annoyed shouts of passing motorists. We hadn't seen a designated crosswalk anywhere, so we braved the five lanes with awkward shuffles and apologies. There was a myriad of closet-sized sheds propped up on every available square of sidewalk. Each structure was braced with ropes. Some were tied to light posts, some to nails sticking from nearby buildings. Nathan was exactly the wrong height. He caught several ropes with his neck, causing vendors to scream with panic and irritation at the careless foreigner threatening to topple their place of business.

We stumbled into a dark labyrinth of aluminum-covered vendor stalls with a thick stench of garbage, human waste, and rancid meat. We didn't want to insult the shopkeepers who were proudly displaying their sickly, brown, and carious cuts of beef and pork, so we held our breath and suppressed our gag reflexes. When we emerged by the river, the relatively fresh smell of smog and fermenting fish was a pleasant relief. A sweet woman who'd seen us exit the covered market approached us. She fluffed my frizzy hair with a childlike grin on her face while asking if we spoke English. When we admitted that we did, she excitedly explained that we were in luck.

We had arrived on a holiday. It was Buddha Day! For one day only, hiring a tuk tuk was twenty baht (less than a dollar) for all tourists. As tourists on this holiday, we were also eligible for free entry to all temples, and a special government promotion on all travel in Thailand. The woman was thrilled to share her insider knowledge with us. She explained that the Grand Palace was closed in the morning for prayers to Buddha, and the Thai government felt terrible about the inconvenience. To apologize, they had apparently ordered citywide discounts and unparalleled promotions. She flagged down a tuk tuk and gave him quick instructions that we couldn't understand. Then, they did a strange handshake. It was the kind of handshake you might see in a movie, when money is exchanged covertly for small baggies of illegal substances. I didn't think much of it; we knew nothing of Thai culture. It was entirely possible that strange, secretive handshakes were the norm.

After waving goodbye to our anonymous angel, our tuk tuk driver brought us to the tourist information center. We were introduced to a travel agent who confirmed that the government had indeed extended discounted rates for airfare, trains, and busses to all foreigners for Buddha Day. He asked us about our budget, then suggested an itinerary within our price range. Before we could think, we had booked a two-week trip, all expenses prepaid. It included five days on each coast of southern Thailand, a plane flight to the northern mountains of Chiang Mai, and a jungle trek. We were a little hesitant to skip the entire central portion of Thailand, but were told that the best parts of the Kingdom were its tropical southern islands and its northern jungle excursions. Our travel agent suggested we buy visas for Laos, Vietnam, and Cambodia in advance. To get the visas we had to relinquish our passports for a couple of weeks to a man named Loppy. This made us both nervous, but Loppy was an English speaker and very convincingly nonchalant about the whole arrangement. He was confident that we would be able to get on planes and trains and could book hotels without them. He promised that when our trip was done, he would have our passports and visas sent to Chiang Mai. They would be waiting for us when we returned from our jungle trek. It was impossible to tell if we were making a bad decision.

That afternoon, we made our way to the Grand Palace. The kindly woman we had met earlier in the day said that it had been closed for prayer all morning, but strangely, the ticket office attendant knew nothing of this. He said that the palace was open from eight in the morning until five in the afternoon every day. We weren't too concerned about the tidbit of misinformation. It was such a little detail.

The palace was indeed grand. It was our first exposure to the style and size of Thai temples, so we walked through the compound slowly, examining every detail. The unremarkable main gates were a strange contrast to the extravagant decorations within. The sky was pierced a dozen times by the golden needle points of decorative stupas. Every building was bejeweled with colored glass, mirrors, small gems, and gold paint. The Grand Palace was a delicate balance between opulent and gaudy. I wasn't fond of the kitschy decorations, but I couldn't help but be impressed by the palace as a whole. Murals lined many of the inner walls, depicting historical battles with figures carefully painted in silver and green. Golden gargoyles perched on rooftops, holding hands in an unbroken chain, as if to ward evil from their lofty stations.

Nathan and I reached the limits of our sightseeing endurance after two hours of walking through the palace grounds. We made our way back to the street and hired a tuk tuk to bring us to our hostel so we could get cleaned up for dinner and drinks.

When we reached our room, we cranked the air-conditioning unit to full power and took quick showers to rinse away the sweat and grime. Nathan suggested a short nap, to give the sun time to set and the city time to cool. He found no argument with me.

When I woke, I felt incredibly refreshed. I was surprised to find that the sun still hadn't gone down. Then I looked at my watch. "Hey Nathan," I prodded him with my elbow, "take a guess at what time it is."

He groaned from beneath the covers, then peeked out at me. "Why? What's the matter?" When he realized it was light, he threw the covers off of himself and sat up quickly on the edge of the bed.

I answered, "Well, I'm hungry, that's one thing. The other thing is that we accidentally took a sixteen-hour nap."

"No way!" Nathan skipped over to the window, to look out at the street below. It was bustling with morning activities. Shop owners were opening their stalls, uniformed children were walking to school, or being driven on the backs of their parents' mopeds, and traffic was a relentless din of horns and squealing brakes.

Marsupials and Hair Removal

We were both glad to have given ourselves more than one night in Bangkok before heading out on our prepaid trip. We had one more full day before our train departed Bangkok Central Station, heading south. A good night's rest had rejuvenated us, but it was exhausting just to think about venturing back out into the city. Every moment threatened to overload our senses. A thousand new sights and smells bombarded us. Every task took colossal effort because we were constantly on guard, trying to keep track of a million things we didn't understand. We had trouble doing the simplest things. We didn't know how to order food at a street vendor. When someone ordered it for us, we didn't know how to eat it, or what it was. We couldn't barter with a taxi driver because we didn't know how much our money was worth, or how far we wanted to go. We couldn't ask for a bathroom when we had to use one, then we couldn't use one when we found it because we didn't have toilet paper or running water. Being a backpacker was draining, but we didn't want to miss out on anything, so we pushed ourselves into one uncomfortable and confusing situation after another.

We decided to spend our morning at a specialty market called Chatuchak. We had heard about it from another guest at our hostel. He promised that we would be able to find *anything* under the Southeast Asian sun, including an adorable creature called a sugar glider. I didn't know much about sugar gliders, except that they were supposedly the cutest marsupials on the planet.

I wanted one. Nathan laughed at the idea because he thought I was kidding.

We found a bus stop near our hostel and stood waiting for a bus with the number thirty-seven written on it, which our hostel receptionist had suggested we take, to get to Chatuchak. Several passed before we realized we would have to flag the bus down for it to stop. We finally got one, paid our seven cents, and hoped that the market would be obvious, because we had no idea how to express our final destination to the driver. We had nothing to worry about. The market was enormous. The guy who told us about it hadn't been exaggerating when he said we would be surprised by the selection. We saw virility aids, owls, clothes, car parts, obscene wooden carvings, dogs (for eating), curtains, mopeds, lizards, taxidermy supplies, and sugar gliders, to name a few things. We wandered through the labyrinth of vendor stalls on narrow dirt paths until we found the gliders. They were housed in metal bird cages, five or six to a cage. They looked like a miniature blend between koala bears and squirrels with long and highly coordinated tails. One could fit easily into the palm of my hand. I excitedly pulled Nathan closer, "Nathan, are they as cute as you imagined?"

He was bending to squint into the tiny brown eyes of an unusually sociable glider, who was clinging to the side of the cage. "You know, I hadn't really imagined their cuteness."

I wasn't listening to his answer. I was daydreaming about the pouch I would knit for my glider. I was sure I could knit something comfortable and safe, something that I could hang from my belt. They were even cuter than I thought possible, the cuddliest living creatures. "Kittens and puppies don't hold a candle to these things," I mused, half to myself, half to Nathan. I was all in. I asked the saleswoman how much they cost. As I was converting the amount from baht into U.S. dollars, Nathan realized that I was serious.

"For a measly fifty dollars, I could buy evolutionary perfection. They're beautiful," I told Nathan, excitedly.

Nathan pulled me several steps from the woman selling them to try to talk some sense into me. "This is a terrible idea. I agree that they're amazing, but…" Nathan stopped mid-sentence. He rolled his eyes toward the saleswoman, who was explaining the ins and outs of raising a sugar glider to another potential customer.

She was saying, "We sell them young. It's critical to allow time for the bond to form between owner and glider. They need to be fed every two hours around the clock, from an eye dropper. They have a high-pitched screech, which they are not shy about using to express discomfort of any kind. They sleep during the day and scream through most of the night. They also like to mark their owner with their scent, which is usually quite offensive, but a very good sign because it means the bond is forming."

I realized my mouth was hanging open when the saleswoman started staring at me over the shoulder of the man she was addressing. I smiled at her before looking back to Nathan. "Is she serious? Why would anyone buy a pet that required so much attention? These things sound like more work than a human infant."

Nathan sighed with relief.

Sugar gliders were much more than I was prepared to handle for the pleasure of their insanely adorable company. Nathan also reminded me that our two-week travel plan included a plane ride. It was highly doubtful that the Thai TSA would be willing to let me on a plane with one of these things.

We made our way back to the city by train, empty handed. Instead of finding a tuk tuk from the train station back to our hostel, we decided to walk there by way of Chinatown.

I was torn between wanting to cry from exhaustion and wanting to skip down every street, exploring shops, interacting with locals, and taking pictures of every strange thing I saw. It was only early afternoon, but it felt as though we had been away from our hostel for days. I could tell Nathan felt the same drag, so I suggested a cold beer, and a relaxing dinner on the way home.

He nodded his head weakly, "That sounds incredible. I need to sit down."

With something to look forward to, we made our way more quickly toward Chinatown. Hundreds of red lanterns hung from every light post and on strings suspended from one side of the street to the other. There were thousands of people flowing in both directions through a densely packed covered market. We found ourselves drawn into the confusion. About seventy-eight percent of the items being sold were completely unrecognizable to us. The market was crammed so tightly with people and goods that we couldn't move without full body contact with strangers. We were incredulous when we heard the revving of a motorcycle engine close behind. Nathan pulled me out of the way just as a motorist wearing a tinted helmet pushed his bike through the river of shoppers. I couldn't imagine what the biker was thinking. It was equivalent to driving a motorcycle through a grocery store to avoid stoplights. Madness. No one else seemed annoyed or surprised by his bold behavior.

A few shops displayed tables piled high with brightly colored dried fruits, nuts, and fresh vegetables. I wanted to take pictures of the vibrant colors and carefully placed goods but couldn't reach my pockets without molesting someone behind me. I thought I saw intestines perched on one man's scales, but Nathan was certain the same item was a brain. He also claimed he saw bright pink stomachs that looked just like the ones in Pepto-Bismol commercials. I thought the same pink globs were cookies.

We escaped the market's mayhem onto a street lined with women, each sitting on her own stool, with a spool of thread and a small bowl of white, chalky liquid by her side. I watched as one of them slathered the chalky liquid onto her customer's cheeks. She rubbed the thread aggressively over the woman's whitish skin, yanking out hairs as she went. While I stood gawking, another of these hair-removal specialists spotted me. I don't know if she shot up a flare or made some quick phone calls, but I was instantly the focus of everyone's attention. Apparently, it was obvious that I was in need of some help. Nathan stood transfixed as tiny Chinese women flocked around me, touching the hairy places on my skin while making grotesque faces. I was perfectly content having cheek hairs and crazy eyebrows, but that didn't stop them. They waved their chalk and torture strings before my panicked eyes as if they were dangling lifelines. If I hadn't been so worried about an unwelcome demonstration by one of these crazed women, I might have been embarrassed that so much attention was being paid to my facial hair, especially in front of my new boyfriend.

I spun in place trying to locate Nathan, hoping for some help. He was standing several feet away from me. My pleading only made his grin widen. "Nathan! Get me out of here! These women are like a pack of wolves."

"What do you mean? You're making friends. This is a cultural experience."

I smirked wickedly, "I'm about to give *you* a cultural experience." I got the attention of the nearest five women and made a show of pointing at Nathan's arm hair, then made a disgusted face of my own. I encouraged them to help me clean him up and make him smooth. The tides quickly turned, as women raced toward Nathan.

He was much more willing to get moving when he realized he was no longer an innocent bystander.

We made our way to Kao San Road, Bangkok's backpacker haven, for dinner and beers. For dessert, I ate my first insect, a grasshopper. It could have easily passed as a French fry in any American fast-food joint, minus the legs. Nathan couldn't manage eye contact while I chewed, but later that evening, he one-upped me by eating multiple bites of a durian fruit. Durian is the flavor of rotten onion mixed with pudding the color and consistency of pus, with a hint of dirty feet. Nathan ate four or five bites of this stuff. I could only stomach one. It's illegal to sell it in certain markets because of its putrid smell. It's just as illegal to carry durian onto a plane as it is to carry an AK-47. I would almost rather be trapped on a plane with an AK-47-toting psychopath than a durian. At least with a gun the end would be quick. With a durian on board, I would suffer terribly and perhaps permanently. The smell seeps into one's skin and lingers in the bloodstream.

To top off the evening, we found a fish massage parlor, and put our feet into a tank of water filled with tiny, shockingly aggressive and hungry fish.

Massage is sort of a misnomer. In reality, we paid to be attacked by a tank of flesh-eating monstrosities with a taste for dead skin. It tickled until it didn't. Nathan was convinced that the carnivorous massaging fish were trying to kill him. To be fair, they did seem to want to eat him more than anyone else. They chewed relentlessly on his ankles. He sat enduring it uncomfortably until he started to bleed. These tanks are everywhere, and most tourists try them at least once. It's easy to tell when you're within fifty feet of one of them because you can hear squealing laughter intermingled with fear and panic.

Instead of paying for a tuk tuk or a taxi, we walked from Kao San Road back to our hostel. It was past midnight when we finally reached our room. I packed my things for our early morning departure while Nathan crawled into bed. His backpack lay empty on the floor; his things were scattered around the room in disarray.

I went to bed that night with a sense of accomplishment. We were getting the hang of things. Bangkok was less intimidating every minute. I slightly regretted our decision to depart the city with such haste. Our two-week prepaid journey was going to send us south, then north, skipping much of central Thailand.

Thai Travel

The next morning, I woke Nathan earlier than I said I would. He had disagreed with me about what time we needed to get up, to catch our train. Instead of arguing, I took advantage of his morning confusion and the fact that he didn't own a watch. At my urging, he groggily stumbled around our room, picking up his things and shoving them carelessly into the bottom of his backpack. When we reached the train station, he noticed that the giant clock above the ticket counter read 0700. He nudged my arm with his elbow, "Wow, we made great time this morning. I told you getting up at six forty-five would be early enough."

I couldn't have asked for a better lead-in. "Six forty-five is the time that you suggested we set the alarm for. I thought that was ludicrous, so set our alarm for five forty-five instead."

Nathan scowled. "You woke me up at five forty-five? Look how early we are. We could have slept another fifteen minutes!"

I glared at his glassy eyes and suggested we grab a cup of coffee with our extra time. He didn't argue with that. We found ourselves a few snacks for the eight-hour ride, then boarded a train to a town called Suritani. We were told that in Suritani, there would be a ferry to take us to our hotel on Koh Phangan Island, which floated several hours from the western coast of southern Thailand. Just as the train pulled away from the station, a twinge of uneasiness reminded me that we were leaving without our passports.

It didn't take us long to realize that the Thai people have tourism figured out. It's difficult to comprehend how they so elegantly manage so many high-strung, irritatingly organized, compulsively schedule-following visitors. When you book a trip with a tourism office, they hand you an envelope. Inside is a single piece of paper with so little information it's laughable.

7 a.m.-hotel pick up

4 p.m.-arrive at new hotel

Sure, this might seem like enough information if you are planning to take a single bus for eight hours, from the door of one hotel to the door of another, but what this paper fails to mention is that you will be picked up at 7 AM by a tuk tuk. The tuk tuk will deliver you to the train station. The train will drop you off in the center of a small town where a van is waiting. You will be pushed into the van with a dozen other people. That van will drive for twenty minutes, then stop on the side of a deserted highway. You will be asked to get out. When you disembark, everyone will receive a sticker on his or her shirt sleeve. The colors of these stickers will not be the same for all tourists on board. You will be handed your bag and the van will drive away. This is when most tourists start to panic. I have to admit, there's something devilishly entertaining about watching strangers experience meltdowns.

Next, a bus will stop and a man will hop off. He will take all the people with pink stickers and tell the green and blue-stickered people to stay put. Then a moped will stop and take the one blue sticker man. You will be shoved onto another passing bus, loaded with fellow green-sticker tourists. You will be told to get off at the next stop and switch to the bus with the word *Pen* on its back fender. A man waiting on the bus will take the sticker off of your shirt and scribble his name onto a piece of paper, before handing it to you. He'll say, "Don't lose this."

Your day will continue with similar exchanges until you arrive at the door of another hotel. The entire operation is seamless.

On our first night at our new hotel in Koh Phangan, we spent some time at the bar, unwinding and getting to know some of our fellow travelers. We were asked four separate times if we were Canadian. I turned to Nathan and asked, "Do we look Canadian? Why is everyone asking if we are?"

Nathan explained that according to the international community, asking a stranger who speaks English if they are American is the equivalent of asking a chubby woman if she's pregnant. It's an insult to non-Americans, so most people ask if you're Canadian instead, especially if they like you. They can't imagine liking an American. We enjoyed a couple of drinks with a French couple, Fredrick and Elise, who had also assumed we were Canadian.

They informed us that we wouldn't be able to rent mopeds to explore the island because we were without our passports, a fact which concerned them deeply. They didn't say so, but we could tell they felt sorry for us and thought we were in serious trouble. We were a little disappointed at the news, but being so new to Thailand, it was probably better we didn't jump into the moped rental game so soon. The bartender told us that if a taxi goes out of control and hits your rent-a-moped while it's parked on the street, you are responsible for the full cost of the bike and any damages his taxi may have sustained. There is logic at the core of this system. The accident would never have happened if you hadn't decided to visit Thailand. It holds up in court.

Before going to bed, we made plans to meet Fredrick and Elise for another drink the next evening. The following morning, we woke early for a snorkeling, kayaking, and mountain trekking trip in the Angthong Marine Park. It was an exhausting excursion, partly because of all the activity, but also because it rained for ten hours straight. We returned to our room soggy and chilled to the bone, but excited to meet up with our new friends. When we got to the bar, Fredrick began a twenty-minute recounting of his first Thai massage experience. Massages are a trademark of the tourism business in Thailand. Women set up shop on street corners, on beaches, in hotel lobbies, and inside your suitcase if you leave it unattended for more than three minutes. You can expect a chorus of, "Helloooooo! Massssssaaaaggggeee!" wherever you go. These women charge two to five dollars an hour for their services. Most foreigners find this price so enticing they lose all ability to think rationally. Anyone thinking rationally would see the red flags flying. Namely, that there is no possible way that these women have any formal training. The only way three million women could have the credentials to perform chiropractic bone cracking would be if elementary schools had included massage instruction as part of their curriculum since the 1940s. This discrepancy, according to Fredrick, becomes apparent the moment their coconut-oiled fingers grip your body. He explained his afternoon massage in detail, beginning with an animated imitation of the elbow-drop move. This was the move that his four-foot, elderly masseuse had used to incapacitate him. Rendered helpless, he had remained on her bamboo table for an hour, blindly enduring her jump-pounce-grind moves. He showed no embarrassment while confessing that tears had been running down his cheeks as his mouth hung open, unable to protest. The old woman hadn't known much about massage, but Fredrick was convinced that she had formal training in hand-to-hand combat.

"Somehow ze angry fingers, she used zem to paralyze my voice. My vocal cords. Shit. I wuz at her mercy, completely." For some reason, Fredrick's thick French accent made the story doubly enjoyable. Maybe it was the underlying desire we all have to see the French suffer, just a little. Whatever it was, Fredrick had Nathan and me laughing so hard we cried. Despite his story, Fredrick admitted that he and Elise would continue to receive their three-dollar massages for the duration of their trip. It was too cheap to pass up. I understood completely. Having spent eighty dollars on a massage in the U.S., I couldn't resist the opportunity to get one for three dollars, no matter how bad it was.

Fredrick's story had an altogether different effect on Nathan. It was all he needed to hear on the subject to decide, with conviction, that he was not even remotely interested in trying it. Ever. I attempted without success for several days to change his mind. It wasn't until about a week later, when he came across an article, referring to a women's prison in Chiang Mai, that the topic of massage resurfaced. The article mentioned a rehabilitation program in northern Thailand. Women convicted of crimes with sentences less than life had the option of being rehabilitated to join the workforce. Naturally, massage was the profession they were taught. Inexplicably, the only thing Nathan pulled from this story was that these women had been trained by experienced, professional masseurs. That gave them credibility. It gave them his trust. I couldn't believe he was less afraid of women who had committed potentially violent crimes than he was of untrained grandmothers.

Grifter Nation

We stayed on Koh Phangan for a few days, then took a ferry to Koh Samui, another island paradise on the same coast. It was during our stay on Koh Samui that we uncovered a form of patriotism so expertly camouflaged, so seemingly innocent, that it suckers countless travelers from all over the world every day. Even we had fallen into the clutches of the con. The scam goes something like this:

You arrive in Bangkok on a Sunday morning with a place to stay, but no plans. You decide to take a stroll down a chaotic street with a name you sound ridiculous trying to pronounce.

Fact: You are a walking target.

A sixty-year-old woman approaches. She is an English speaker with a smile and a mouthful of compliments. In a word, adorable. She lets you in on a secret. Today is a special government-sponsored holiday, Buddha Day. Until 2 p.m. all tuk tuks are only twenty baht, temples aren't charging entrance fees and the tourism offices are required to give discounted rates. She shows you a map and points to the only tourism office in the city run by the government. She flags down a tuk tuk and gives him a list of places to take you. She winks at him and awkwardly shakes his hand. He is secretly handing her a sizable kickback for her part in the shakedown. Off you go! The driver delivers you as promised to a couple of fantastic temples, then to the tourism office where you book a two-week adventure. The price seems too good to be true, by American standards.

Fact: There is no such thing as Buddha Day.

Like us, you don't realize until days, weeks, maybe months later that you've been had. Other travelers mention their extreme luck in Bangkok, in passing. They marvel at the odds, how they managed to pick, unknowingly, the perfect day to arrive in the city. Buddha Day! A day when all temple prices are reduced, and the tourism offices are required to lower their rates as an act of good faith toward tourists from all over the globe.

You smile and tell them that you must have been in Bangkok the same day as they were. What a coincidence! Then the details begin to emerge. They were in Bangkok three weeks before you even left the United States. The couple across the room also hit Buddha Day and they were in Bangkok two months ago.

People who received help from strangers, information about Buddha Day, suggestions for places to visit, cheap vacations, etc., start speaking up. All seduced by the same intricate scheme. It is hard to be angry at discovering such an organized, efficient, nationwide, publicly perpetrated hoodwink.

You've been had, but *wow*.

Any country that can convince every demographic, every member of the populace, that it is in their own self-interest to aid in a national scam, in their own self-interest to lie, to spend time tricking total strangers into believing in a fake holiday, *wow*. I respect the sheer number of participating parties. An entire nation of grifters.

Our situation wasn't all bad. We spent hundreds less than a couple of girls we met from New Zealand, and compared to prices elsewhere in the world, we were still sitting pretty-pretty cheap.

Before Koh Samui, I had never heard the words "lady" and "boy" condensed to form the single, accurately descriptive word, "ladyboy." Maybe I was naive. I was certainly naive about the nature of several other forms of entertainment we discovered in Thailand. I got my first real, local information about ladyboys in the islands. A woman working the bar at our hotel explained that things got crazy around 3 a.m. every morning because tourists are at their weakest. The ladyboys lay in wait, all day if they must, for this moment. The moment every twenty-two-year-old man develops a blood alcohol-induced blind spot, a blind spot for Adam's apples. You almost have to see it to believe it, but if you do see it, you'll wish you hadn't. Macho weightlifters with mean tattoos and spikes poking from their neck skin turn into helpless victims to these lovely boys. Boys ranging from beautiful seductresses to pimple-faced pubescents wearing skinny jeans and terrible wigs. If it didn't drum up so much business, I would have taken offense to the commonly accepted notion that the only thing tourists use to determine sex is the length of one's hair. In fact, that does seem to be the only way the 3 a.m. crowd makes decisions about whom to sneak back to their hotel room.

No one ever complains the next morning about their company. I am therefore led to believe that it either goes unnoticed, or there is a suspension of cultural and social norms for all young men in Thailand, which results in uncharacteristic behavior.

Ladyboys are fascinating. Some of these young men are stunningly beautiful. They are not always involved in the sex industry. Some are performers. They sing, lip sync, dance, and dress up in elaborate costumes. They perform to be admired as beautiful women. I would have loved to talk to one of these boys. Nathan kept trying to figure out where they all went when they got too old to perform or look even remotely like an attractive woman. He made a joke to a chef we met much later on the trip about the curious disappearance of ladyboys. The man took it as an accusation. He felt the need to clarify that the missing fifteen-year window in his resume was due to monk service and nothing else.

In Koh Samui, we also learned a few things about traffic. We determined with minimal effort that all roads were one-way roads, in both directions. Most drivers were indifferent to mortal peril. Occasionally, we would see someone slightly nervous on the roadway, but not often. On our first taxi ride, we passed four cars and five mopeds going fifty on a blind curve. Mopeds were not subject to the same rules as cars. They were allowed to go the wrong way on any street, as long as they were on the shoulder. This may not sound like a big deal, but when a moped driving straight at you, mere inches from the side of your taxi, decides to take a left-hand turn across traffic, it becomes a very big deal.

We were so new to being travelers and so unfamiliar with every local custom that much of our time was spent telling each other things we had noticed. We kept each other laughing with ridiculous stories of our own ignorance and misguided perceptions. One of my favorite Thai customs is the use of respect words. There is one that men use and one that women use to show respect for the people with whom they are speaking. When a man is speaking, after every sentence and sometimes in the middle of them, it is customary for him to use the word *cup*. It is always said quickly and precisely. Women use the word *kaaaah* in the same way, though they speak it slowly and nasally. As far as we could tell, the longer the *kaaaah*, the greater the sincerity. I found it endlessly entertaining to count the number of *cups* and *kaaahs* exchanged in a typical Thai conversation. It would have made a good drinking game.

Naturally, after learning this custom, I began using *kaaaah* to show my respect for Nathan whenever possible.

"Hey Nathan, can you hand me the toothpaste? Kaaaah."

"By the way, Nathan, I hand washed your underwear for you, kaaaah."

He loved it.

On the topic of hand-washing underwear, it became painfully clear that Nathan was not experienced enough to be trusted with the task of washing undergarments. We didn't have access to washing machines on a regular basis, and he had failed to pack a reasonable number of pairs, so I took it upon myself to keep them clean. This was a disturbingly graphic way to get closer as a couple. I don't recommend it. I hid my true feelings about his ineptitude by explaining that washing clothes in the sink was something that occurred below four feet. Therefore, it fell within my domain, according to our division of labor agreement.

We're Canadian

Our prepaid journey took us to a third island in southern Thailand called Phuket. It was on the opposite coastline, which meant we had to travel over the mainland to reach it. The day we transferred from Koh Samui to Phuket was a wild one. The entire journey took thirteen hours, required four modes of transportation, and resulted in a little white lie regarding our nationality.

We woke to the angry pounding of fists and possibly a head on our hotel room door. I stumbled to it and peeked out, squinting into the blazing sun. There was a van full of people staring back at me. The man who stood between the bus and my face, much closer to the latter than the former, leaned close enough to lick my forehead and screamed, "The van is waiting!"

I was temporarily frozen in sleepy confusion. Why was a strange man yelling at my eyebrows?

Neither of us had bothered to look at our pickup time for the transfer to Phuket. It had all gone so smoothly thus far that we had gotten a little lazy. Our departure was twenty minutes past due.

I have never packed so quickly in my entire life. Packing quickly is not something I do. Ever. My hair was sticking straight out on the left side of my head and tangled flat on the right. I could have easily used electrocution or head trauma as an excuse for our stupidity, but I was too tired to think that clearly. My eyes were half closed, I had terrible morning breath, and my shirt managed to end up backwards. We made it out the door in about four minutes. I don't even know what Nathan was doing while I was throwing things, unplugging electronics, and cursing our unpreparedness. I went from deep sleep to a crowded van full of Nigerians in less than five minutes. With a series of groggy attempts to use my French-Canadian accent, I hoped to imply our Canadian-ness, "Early morning eh?", "Cramped bus, eh?", "Sorry to make ya wait, eh." Frazzled, confused, out of breath, hoping not to have forgotten anything vital, I looked over at Nathan, "What the…?"

It was like looking into a snow globe of peace and tranquility. If I hadn't been certain that he too just experienced the previous five minutes of chaos, I would have sworn that he had just finished a satisfying cup of tea and a twenty-minute meditation session. He was totally calm. There was an ever-so-slight grin on his face. He turned to meet my questioning gaze.

"What, you're not used to this kind of morning?" He continued, "I wake up like this every morning."

I was astounded, dazzled even, by his ability to live in a state of entropic Zen. He thrived in chaos, took comfort in its familiarity. He dodged life's bullets with ease. I didn't understand it. He was like a car accident that I couldn't help watch, maybe because I knew he would always climb out of the wreckage unharmed.

When the man sitting behind me asked where we were from, I couldn't bear to admit that we were American after causing such a scene. I felt a certain responsibility to avoid marring America's image while abroad, so I said we were Canadian. It's better to establish your own annoying travel habits rather than having to live up to some preconceived nationality-based expectation. Norwegians are on drugs, thus forgetful. Belgians take themselves too seriously. Canadians are too nice. Americans are self-absorbed and the French suffer from superiority complexes. You catch the drift. It's no fun when some irritating schmuck from your country contaminates the world's opinion of you. I realized I was doing this to all Canadians when I claimed to be one, but I wasn't worried. They're far too nice to do anything about it.

That day we went from van to bus to ferry. On the ferry, I saw one of my favorite signs of all time. It read,

1. Follow safety regulations.
2. Do not move around in confusion.

Clearly the operator of that boat had tourists figured out. Sometimes things get pretty confusing, and when they do, we tourists tend to walk around looking for answers. We would be much less of a bother if we just sat down until the confusion passed.

When we arrived at the ferry terminal, a bus was waiting. We boarded and settled in for a five-hour ride. Just as a sign reading *Phuket* appeared in the distance, we nailed a pickup truck carrying fifteen people in the back. Our bus crushed the side panel, but miraculously, nothing else. I couldn't see the immediate consequences of the collision, so when Nathan asked, I had to extrapolate.

"We destroyed the truck, but the fifteen people in the back must be acrobats because they all flew into the air and landed on the curb over there." I pointed.

We had little hope of things working out quickly. Traffic stopped. Our bus sat in the middle lane of a five-lane highway with a truck T-boned at the front, waiting for the police. After about twenty minutes, the copilot came to us with whispered promises of expedited escape. Yes, our bus had a copilot. I'm not sure what the job description for this position was, but I didn't really think it was the time to ask. He roped us into a five-dollar ticket in his own private van, which he assured would be at the scene within fifteen minutes. He managed to sell another six people the same deal. We all dug our bags from the bottom of the bus and threw them onto the roof of the 1973 minivan when it arrived. The driver, a man with one lazy eye and a giant hairy mole on his neck, tied them down moderately well before speeding into traffic.

Nathan and I spent the remainder of our journey discussing the phenomenon of the hairy mole in Thailand. We had observed too many to ignore. A typical hairy mole had three to six-inch long, black hairs jutting from the depths of a dark, misshapen skin bulb. At first, we didn't attribute our sightings to anything more than the strange grooming habits of a few individuals. Over time, however, with dozens of sightings and several failed inquiries, we came up with a theory. Mole hairs are lucky in Thailand. Why else would everyone refuse to pull them out or shave them? Nathan had a mole on his arm. It was nothing compared to the local specimens, but it did have two dark hairs growing from it. I insisted that he let them grow. For the remainder of our trip, I checked on them often, and made sure that he took good care of them. Whenever things started to get tough, my first thought was of the mole hairs, whether they had been damaged in some way. They represented our fortune. The longer the hairs grew, the better I felt.

Monkeys Can Rip Your Face Off

I suspected from the very start of our journey that monkeys would make an appearance in our lives. We arrived in Phuket about a week and a half after entering Thailand, at which point, I began to cultivate what I sincerely believed to be a healthy fear of monkey violence in Nathan. I'm not sure where this deeply rooted notion of terrible monkey acts started for me. Maybe it was one too many episodes of *Chimp Eden*, a television program that had impressed upon me how dangerous and unpredictable chimpanzees can be. Maybe it was instinct, my conscious mind manifesting a subconscious and universal truth. Monkeys are dangerous. They can rip your face off. End of story.

Backpack Like You Mean It

1.5 seconds before someone gets their face ripped off.

Over dinner one night, I breached the topic, "Nathan, did you know that monkeys hate it when you wave bananas at them?"

He chuckled. Not the response I had been looking for. I realized I hadn't started a moment too soon. His monkey knowledge was embarrassingly limited. I had my work cut out for me. Two days later while walking on the beach I tried again, "Nathan, monkeys really hate being caught off guard."

He didn't chuckle, just gave a slightly raised eyebrow. Then in the market bargaining for a pair of shorts, "Nathan, monkey mothers are extraordinarily protective of their young, and could kill you before you had time to blink."

His indifference finally cracked, "What? What are you talking about?" He demanded, "Why would a monkey want to kill me?"

I wanted him to ponder this very question. Why indeed? I gave him a couple of minutes to mull it over, then answered, "Nathan, that's the point. Who the hell knows what monkeys are thinking? That's why they're so dangerous. If I knew why monkeys turned lethal without warning and ripped people's faces off in a split second of unbridled rage, I probably wouldn't be so cautious around them."

I wasn't certain my words had any impact until we visited Monkey Beach on Phi Phi Island. It was an insane tourist attraction. I don't mean insane in the sense that it was so awesome that everyone should go there. I mean it was insanity to be within fifty feet of people so idiotic around primates. Tourists willingly entered an enclosed space, to play with animals that could rip their faces off. Our tour boat motored up to a tiny beach. There were a dozen other boats, with two dozen people on each, all crowding a stretch of sand that spanned the length of a backyard swimming pool. Every tourist except me (and begrudgingly, Nathan) jumped off of their respective boat to get a closer look at one of the two hundred monkeys littering the sand, trees, and rocks. People made all the major mistakes. They waved bananas, taunted mothers, and touched babies. I was genuinely surprised that no one was murdered. The tourists fed the monkeys their snacks, shared their sodas, and took close-ups with their seven hundred-dollar cameras.

I sat in the back of the transport van on the way home with a young couple speaking a language I couldn't recognize. If they had been speaking English, I might not have been able to resist the urge to be the voice of reason. A voice they had evidently never heard speak on the topic of monkey safety. I desperately wanted to interrupt their giggling as they relived their exciting home video. Said video featured the man handing an obviously irritated monkey his bottle of coke. I wanted to tell them, "Monkeys hate it when you take videos of them. Did you know that any one of those monkeys could have ripped your face off in about 1.5 seconds?"

It's hard to believe that some people don't even realize when their life is hanging by a thread. I couldn't educate every tourist with a camera, but I was committed to doing my best to keep Nathan safe. It was going to become increasingly difficult. From Phuket, our prepaid vacation package was taking us to Chiang Mai for a jungle trek. I knew what stalked the dark recesses of that jungle. Monkeys. Our jungle trip also came with an elephant ride. Thankfully, I don't have the same completely rational fear of elephants.

Nathan Cuddles Stranger

I was glad to be going to Chiang Mai on a plane instead of braving Thai traffic. We had seen some incredible things on the road. Among other things in Thailand, it is perfectly appropriate to do the following on a moped:

Drink hot coffee
Change a diaper
Carry up to five passengers

> Talk on your cell phone
> Drink a beer
> Yo-yo
> Roll a cigarette
> Make out
> Transport farm animals
> Sell ice-cream
> Perform karaoke

    We arrived in Chiang Mai to discover that our hotel was a shanty. I immediately checked to see if Nathan had plucked his lucky mole hair. It was safe, so I attributed our poor accommodations to probability. We couldn't have expected to escape entirely from hostels that made us uncomfortable. We wouldn't have been legitimate backpackers without spending a little time in rooms that made us itch, gag, break out in hives, or gave us the creeps. Thankfully, we only spent one night in Chiang Mai before being whisked off on our jungle trek through Inathon National Park.
    We were told to wait at our hotel's reception desk for an early morning pickup on the first day of our trek. When the van arrived, we stepped into the back where four others were already seated on benches, which were haphazardly attached to the wheel wells. A couple from Belgium, who spoke French and some English, were opposite Nathan and me. They introduced themselves as Camille and Maxime. Camille was slight, with dirty-blond hair that looked unwashed but neat. Maxime's head was the shape of a pencil eraser, tall and narrow. They both wore dark-rimmed glasses and were quick to join in group conversation. A young woman from Australia was also in the van and introduced herself as Willow. She bore enough of a resemblance to a character from the *Harry Potter* series that she thought it necessary to clarify her non-celebrity status. I was worried that with a name like Willow she might be a handful, but she turned out to be easy going and perfectly normal. Next to Willow sat a Japanese boy named Lux, which I assumed was a

nickname, but never asked. Lux didn't speak much English and was painfully shy when questioned about everything except music. The van drove for several minutes while we all exchanged typical introductory information: where we were from, how long we had been traveling, where we had been, and when we were going home. When we stopped, the driver hopped out and left us locked in the back of the van while he ran into a building. We waited for a very long time. Willow was on the brink of a claustrophobic meltdown when our driver finally returned. He was followed by a jovial Frenchman named Valentine. Valentine jumped into the back of the vehicle and began chatting, as if we were his long-lost childhood friends. His clothes were a delicate balance between French chic and homeless vagabond. He was charismatic and used his natural charm to magically bond the group in a way that few could have done.

The seven of us were joined by a Thai man who insisted we all call him Gun. He informed us that we were stuck with him because he had been assigned to our group as a guide. A long black ponytail hung down to the middle of his back, and though he looked strong, he didn't stand much taller than five feet. He spoke easily and understood the nuances of the English language well enough to crack jokes and give us hell when we deserved it.

The trip began with a five-hour hike into Inathon Park. Gun impressed us all with his knowledge, taking the time to show us unique flora and fauna along the way. He constructed a hat out of banana leaves and guilted Nathan into wearing it while showing us which ants we could safely eat. The red ants tasted like sweet tarts and as long as you bit down quickly, they didn't sting the inside of your mouth. Even Nathan volunteered to try one.

Gun warned us of the dangers in the jungle. He didn't try to scare us but made sure we were aware of our surroundings. He had a habit of clapping his hands and singing loudly as we walked, a tactic I had seen before, in areas heavy with predators. I whispered covertly to Gun that I was onto him. He smiled sheepishly and admitted that loud noises were often the best offense against catching a poisonous snake or big cat by surprise. I added, "And monkeys, I would imagine."

Gun nodded, then made a point of making eye contact, "I think tigers are *much* more dangerous than monkeys. You don't have to worry about monkeys."

I winked at him knowingly, "I wouldn't say *much* more dangerous, but there's no sense in panicking people."

Gun also told us about the guide business. He professed his superiority as a woodsman in the Chiang Mai area. One of his competitors had hired a guide to lead a two-day hiking trip into the same park we were exploring. The guide had taken a bottle of whiskey with him and had gotten so drunk on the hike that he had become impossibly lost. The six tourists that were with him got a little more than they bargained for: they were stranded for five days in the jungle without shelter, water, and food. They were forced to follow a drunkard in circles as he tried to get them out of the park. Several of them missed flights home. Not surprisingly, they all filed complaints. Gun said that the guide had dropped his tourists off in Chiang Mai, then disappeared altogether. His company was still looking for him, hoping to recover some of the money they had lost in the ordeal.

On our first night, Gun enlisted the help of a young man from a Karin village not far from our campsite. They were obviously close friends, but the Karin boy didn't speak a lick of English or Thai. He spoke his tribal language, then used sign language and laughing to communicate everything else. He had an impersonation of Smeagol from the *Lord of The Rings* that could have earned him an Academy Award. It got scary after I taught him how to say, "My precious." He was also a strong proponent of drinking cobra blood and whiskey at a fifty-fifty ratio. He managed to convey with theatrics that he believed the concoction could make him invincible. Invincibility seemed like a prerequisite for spending time with him. In the dim orange light of our evening fire, Smeagol told us that he could throw knives. I didn't see him grab the blade at his belt, but thankfully Nathan did. He pulled me out of the way just as a knife flew through the dark and bounced off of its intended target to hit the spot that would have been my rib cage. A couple of throws narrowly missed Nathan as well, so we thought it best to call it an early night. Better asleep than dead.

That night in the frigid darkness of our communal cabin, Nathan accidentally sleep-cuddled Lux. He claimed it was an easy mistake because Lux had smooth skin and a small frame. If Lux woke up during the incident, he had the decency to pretend it never happened. That same night a rat stole my fruit stash, digested it, then delivered it to my pillow. I woke up with sticky rodent droppings clinging to the hair at the nape of my neck.

The trek included another day of hiking, several waterfalls, elephant riding, and on the last day, bamboo rafting. The rafting trip was unexpectedly one of the highlights. By the time our group reached our final activity, we were a tight-knit crew. We split up to occupy two bamboo rafts. Nathan, Valentine, and I were on one raft while Camille, Maxime, Willow, and Lux were on another. Each raft was driven by a pole-wielding guide who sat at the front, pushing off of rocks and the river bottom to keep us moving safely downriver. Our rafts were simple constructions made from five bamboo trees, each about nine inches wide and twelve feet long, lashed together with twine. They floated just above the surface and provided almost no protection from the splashing water. About halfway through the float, the river became rough with rocks and small rapids. This was Valentine's cue to step up. He stole the guide's pole, broke it in half and handed one piece to Nathan, who was seated at the back. Valentine shushed the guide's protests and asked him to sit down and rest while his passengers took a turn. The guide finally relented with a fit of laughter as Valentine nearly toppled from his perch at the bow. When he had regained his balance, he began barking out instructions to Nathan with his thick French accent, "Nay-tan pleeez, stand up! It's zee Titanic, shit man! Help me!"

Nathan stood, struggling to keep his feet while pushing his half-pole on the bank to keep from crashing into it. Ahead, the river narrowed to a small channel between two large rocks, followed by a three-foot drop. I was sitting in the center of the raft, caught between Valentine, who was frantically waving his pole in the air, and Nathan, who was screaming for Valentine to *stop* waving his pole in the air. Nathan strained to keep the raft on course, but without Valentine helping in the front, there was little he could do. Valentine's screams grew louder.

"Nay-tan, I can't save uz! Zee what-er iz too strong. It iz you. You must save uz!"

I could see past Valentine's flailing arms that we were not going to hit the channel. We were heading straight for one of the rocks. Nathan was too busy to notice this, and so was caught off guard by the impact. Valentine had the good sense to crouch down for greater stability just before the violent collision, but Nathan was on two feet when our raft met the stone. He flew headfirst, arms stretched wide, from the back of the raft to the front. The next thing any of us knew, Nathan's face was hanging from the side of the raft and his body was a crumpled heap at Valentine's feet. Valentine stood, looked down at Nathan and said, "Nay-tan, shit. What az appened? Dat waz crazy."

The others had been in the raft right behind us. As we regrouped, still pinned between the rocks and the rushing rapids, they passed us gracefully and slid through the channel. They were all grabbing their stomachs, howling with laughter. Our guide stood, shaking his head, and took Valentine's pole while motioning for him to sit back down.

The rest of the journey was uneventful. We were transported from our river landing back to Chiang Mai. I was sad to say goodbye to our new friends but hoped we might bump into some of them again someday.

Thai massage. If it doesn't hurt, she's doing it wrong.

Prisoners of Prisoners

The morning after our return to Chiang Mai, we started to worry more seriously about our passports. Loppy said they would be waiting upon our return, but the receptionist only shook his head when we asked if there was a package for either of us. We couldn't bring ourselves to do anything about the problem, because that would mean admitting that we were in trouble. Instead, we tried to distract ourselves by exploring Chiang Mai.

Much to Nathan's dismay, I remembered his suggestion to spend some time with the women of the Chiang Mai Correctional Facility.

We invited Willow to join us for an afternoon massage (safety in numbers). Our massages from prisoners-in-training could not have turned out better, at least for me. Nathan was a little worse for wear after the encounter.

The final move, in a true Thai massage, requires the linking of one's fingers behind their head.

I was amused by the irony.

Once in this position, unsuspecting tourists are rolled onto their masseuse's knees as she grinds her elbows into their spine. I heard most of my bones crack, but I regularly pop and snap my joints, so for me, the experience was satisfying. From the room next to mine, I heard Nathan gasp in surprise. He was caught unprepared by his slender, but strong masseuse, and instead of relaxing, he fought as she flipped him over and bent him in half.

I heard the woman working on him giggle as he groaned in pain and surprise. I could tell by the way his moans escalated into high pitched whimpers that his masseuse was working through some aggression issues. When we were finally released, the three of us walked back to our hostel through the blistering heat. Nathan's left arm hung limp at his side. I held his dead, left hand and said, "You were right Nathan. Those women were excellent. I could tell they had gone through a rigorous training program."

When we walked through the door of our hostel, we were examined carefully by the receptionist. He asked us to follow him. We were brought into a back room and handed an envelope each. I opened mine slowly, not knowing what to expect.

I was shocked and relieved to discover my passport, wrapped neatly in white paper with a note scratched hastily on one side. It said, *'Hope you had a good trip. - Loppy.'*

I turned to Nathan. He was holding his passport reverently, staring down at its blue cover.

I smacked him on the arm, "Can you believe it? We actually got them back. This is incredible. How did Loppy do it?"

The receptionist looked confused. He couldn't understand why we seemed so relieved, so excited. He had been told that we were expecting our passports. Our reactions said otherwise. Before he became too suspicious, we thanked him and ran up to our room, triumphant.

We spent the next day with pen and paper, good maps, which incidentally took most of the morning to find, and a general idea of what we were hoping to do next. We had come to the firm conclusion that we wouldn't turn into the kind of traveler we saw loitering on Kao San Road, in Bangkok. The people who hopped from one tourist trap to the next, buying souvenirs, drinking too much, and eating pizzas and burgers at every meal.

Judging by the sheer number of this type of backpacker, the transition from regular person to internationally recognized, grease-sucking vagrant was a slippery slope. We didn't want any part of it, so we made a promise. We promised ourselves that we would do whatever it took to see more and do more than other travelers. We vowed to love every minute of it, no matter what. The experience largely depended on us, how we chose to react to the endless cultural discomfort, lack of privacy, and generally chaotic lifestyle we were living. That evening at dinner, we decided to backpack like we meant it. We clinked Chang beer bottles and congratulated ourselves on our future accomplishments.

Once our path had been vaguely decided, we let our Changs lead the discussion. I began, "Don't you think it's ridiculous how concerned everyone was about our relationship? We've been having an amazing time. So far, there's been absolutely nothing to worry about."

"The only thing we've even disagreed about was how early we needed to be for a train." Nathan agreed.

"I know! Sure, we've discovered some strange things about each other, but that's just bringing us closer."

Nathan's eyebrow went up, "What things have you discovered?"

"Well, for starters you believe that toothbrushes are communal property."

"Oh."

"For the record, they are *not*. I also find it a little odd that you can't remember anything that happens before ten in the morning."

"I'm not a morning person."

"Clearly. You also can't hit a toilet bowl before eight thirty to save your life."

"Well, I find it a little weird that you insist on packing your bag the night before we leave a hotel. Totally naked."

"Hey, there's a good reason for that. If I'm wearing clothes, I can't pack everything where it needs to go. Dirty clothes go at the bottom, and if I'm wearing them, they're dirty. Are you telling me that you mind?"

"No."

"I didn't think so. I'm getting another Chang. Want one?"

Of course, he did. Chang is Thailand's cheap beer. It's everywhere. A liter bottle costs about a dollar fifty. The neat thing about ordering a Chang is that its alcohol content is unpredictable. If the bottle didn't fill properly somewhere along the production line, and more often than not this was the case, it was topped off with whiskey. I was the victim of overconfidence a couple of times. Our first night in Chiang Mai, I had two beers. Nathan also had two beers. When I discovered with utter satisfaction that Nathan was hammered, and I was untouched, I ruthlessly belittled him for his weak little liver. He took it with grace, but the next weekend when I drank a single Chang and barely made it out of the restaurant, he was sure to return the derision.

The plan we had hatched while enjoying our freedom and our Chang, involved something a bit more challenging than an organized trip. We decided to use our passports for what they were *really* good for in Southeast Asia: convincing people we were rich enough *and* stupid enough to take on the responsibility of renting mopeds. For our first renting experience, we minimized our risk by going to a moped dealership. Not many people were willing to offer any form of insurance, but by paying slightly more for two 125 cc bikes, we were given a minimal liability policy. We were told that two bikes with insurance would cost seven dollars a day. I had been in Thailand long enough to know that nothing was worth what anyone said it was. Most things were worth less than sixty percent of their asking price. When Mami, the only English-speaking rental agent, said that our bikes would be seven dollars a day, I dutifully performed the act of demonstrating my incredulity and deep insult at such an unfair price.

Apparently, this act was not perfected, because Mami rolled her eyes, gently put down the stack of papers she needed us to sign, and took a deep breath. She had likely seen Westerners do this a hundred times, a thousand, and every time, if this was any indication, calmly explained that one does not bargain at a dealership in Thailand. One pays.

She seemed credible, so I smiled politely and signed the contract. I could tell Nathan was relieved. He did not enjoy the process of bargaining as I did. He claimed to be more exhausted after half an hour of shopping than a fifteen-mile run. He hated the awkward dance between buyer and seller. I didn't find it awkward at all. It was an enjoyable process that usually resulted in some good laughs. People loved it when I explained how little money I had. Because I was a foreigner, the story of my poverty did little to convince anyone that I couldn't afford their prices, but it did usually buy me an entertainment discount.

Other methods for earning the entertainment discount that did not involve a highly unlikely story of my suffering involved humor. For example, when I made a guy selling lotus seeds laugh so hard, he almost peed his pants, he was much more willing to give me a decent price. How did I do this? I pretended that I had never before seen a lotus seed. I pulled out a piece of paper and a pen and drew the lotus seed hatching into a prehistoric bird-creature. When the man looked up in total confusion, I continued the performance by miming a prehistoric bird-creature attack, waving my arms and punching the air until a crowd started to form around his lotus seed cart. Nathan got as far away from me as he could get. The vendor laughed with friends and strangers alike at how crazy and unstable foreigners are, all the while tossing lotus seeds into a plastic baggie. With the attention I had brought his business, he could afford to cut me a break, which he did by giving me the price everyone else was paying.

The crazier the act (and actress), the better the result. It was perhaps the trickiest form of bargaining and took many interactions to perfect. It also took a travel partner with patience.

Under Attack

Once our mopeds were arranged, we packed a couple of smaller bags with essentials for a week-long excursion. Our large packs stayed behind in the locked storage closet of a hotel, to which we promised to return. Hotels usually didn't have a problem storing backpacks if it meant they would get your business on the flip side of whatever trip you had planned, assuming you survived. They enjoyed the unspoken bonus of being able to keep and sell your things if you didn't return.

    Mami told us to pick up our rental mopeds at eight on the morning of our departure. We arrived at ten past eight, as a courtesy, to give Mami time to pour herself a cup of coffee. We waited at her desk until eight twenty then asked another employee where she was. He didn't speak much English, but we gathered from the business hours printed on the card he handed us, that her workday didn't even start until nine.

    This sort of misunderstanding was becoming a bit too frequent to be a coincidence. The Thai people had been burned so many times by flakey tourists that they no longer trusted any of them to show up when they were supposed to. This was frustrating for someone like me. I respect time. I set deadlines. I wake up to alarms and keep track of the minutes. My own personal behavior didn't matter. I was a foreigner, therefore, could not be trusted. Mami had so little confidence in our timeliness that she had told us to pick up our moped one hour before she even reported to work.

    Nathan was thrilled. It gave us time to get coffee and rub the sleep out of our brains. I was irritated at being treated like an irresponsible child.

    While we sat drinking our coffee, Nathan looked past me to the busy street. His eyes went wide, then a grin appeared on his face. "Wow. Look at that infant cutting a melon with a butcher knife. Unsupervised."

    I turned to look, and though the two-year-old wielding a gigantic knife was unnerving, my attention was grabbed by something slightly more so. I gave an irritated grunt, "We can't be trusted to show up on time, but children are trusted to carry butcher knives and shards of glass? Check out *that* infant. She's running across the street with pieces of glass in each hand."

    It was hard to believe the lack of parental supervision. There were days when we saw the frailest toddlers commit every dangerous act our parents and teachers had spent years educating us to avoid. They ran across streets with lollipops in their mouths, didn't look both ways, held scissors in front of their necks, kept knives tucked in their Velcro belts and carried a pack of matches in their diaper pockets. Either the children in Thailand are a lot tougher than American children, or all the warnings I had received as a kid about the dangers of the world were outright lies.

We finished our coffee while marveling at the survival of such careless children, then went back to the dealership. When Mami finally showed up, we signed our contract for six days, two mopeds, two helmets, and no gasoline. Our plan was hazy at best. We started by having our bikes fueled across the street by a woman selling repurposed coke bottles full of gasoline. Gas wasn't something locals needed a store to sell. If they could find somewhat clean soda or water bottles on the side of the road, they had the free raw materials necessary. A little investment in some gas from the nearest pump, or a siphon, screwdriver and the cover of darkness, and they were in business.

We navigated our wobbly new rides through the busy streets of Chiang Mai, searching for the least intimidating way to exit the city. Our goal was a scenic drive around Inathon National Park. It was a beautiful day. The roads had been paved within the decade, the wind was in our hair and the sun on our faces. We lazily wandered our way through the countryside, stopping often to appreciate scenic lookouts. We rode over rolling hills, through vast stretches of untouched jungle, and stopped to greet children whenever we could. We tasted the sweet freedom of independent tourism. When the thrill of our own liberation wore off, it was dusk. We were riding through clouds of enormous jungle bugs with zero chance of making it to our intended destination. We couldn't even remember the name of the town we had been driving to.

We stopped to ask for directions in a town called Mae Rim. I mimed our situation to an older woman selling hot tea at a roadside shack. She was amused by my performance. She seemed equally amused that Nathan was paying such rapt attention to my enthusiastic display. She must have wondered how someone traveling *with* me could also require a theatrical performance to decipher my needs. Nathan smiled pleasantly, nodding occasionally at particularly clear conceptual demonstrations as she chuckled. She made a couple of cups of hot tea and pushed us onto a bench. While we sipped, we discussed whether she had understood anything I had been trying to communicate. Nathan assured me that certain points had been crystal clear. She ignored us to make several phone calls. Ten minutes later she was still on the phone. She became flustered when we stood to get back on our mopeds in search of a more productive interaction. After all, it was getting dark. My lack of night vision and general lack of skill at operating motorized vehicles had Nathan worried. Just as we were starting our engines, a man on a moped rolled up to the shack. We were able to deduce from the woman's frantic gesticulating that this man knew something we needed to know. With much ado, he conveyed his intention to bring us to a place we could sleep. He walked his moped past us and waved us to follow as he puttered off.

    It turned out as well as we could have hoped. The man we followed was the sole employee of a chic, rustic resort on the top of a nearby mountain. Its long, winding driveway was located less than a quarter of a mile from the tea shack. We trailed behind as he zipped up a gravel path about two feet wide, at full throttle. In a panic at seeing the slope of the path, I accidentally up shifted. My moped instantly stalled, and I watched in horror as Nathan and the mystery man rode off into the jungle ahead of me. It would be a conservative estimate to say that the drive was slanted at a sixty-degree angle. It felt like trying to drive up a wall. I clenched the brakes of my moped hoping not to roll backwards or tip over while attempting to start the engine. When I reached the top, my irritation at having been left in the dust was replaced with awe. I joined Nathan, who was standing slack jawed in front of a beautifully constructed cabin. Its teak and bamboo structure balanced on stilts and overlooked a jungle valley. No one else was staying at the resort, so we were able to strike a hard bargain. We paid ten dollars for the night plus an extra dollar for the delivery of two beers.

Before drinking our beers, we took a little walk through the jungle. It was light enough to navigate in the open, but beneath the canopy, the evening sky disappeared, and we were swallowed by the darkness. In hindsight, it wasn't a great time to be walking through the jungle.

I was intently studying a bug on the ground when Nathan tried to get my attention. I ignored him and whispered, "Hey, look at this crazy beetle. It's almost glowing!" Nathan grabbed me and pointed to a spot a hundred feet from us. The noise and the falling banana trees made me wonder if we were living our last moments together. Something was coming loud and fast, right for us. Nathan was frighteningly calm. He quietly and very sweetly whispered back, "I think we might want to be more concerned about whatever *that* is."

I didn't need encouragement to move with haste to the safety of our cabin.

When we had first seen our beautiful bamboo stilt-cabin in the romantic light of dusk, we hadn't bothered to examine it for one crucial quality, its ability to keep out bugs. It became apparent almost immediately that leaving the lights on in the cabin was an awful idea. The floorboards were not even remotely airtight. They were close enough to keep us from falling through but did little else in the way of protecting us. We decided to keep the porch light on as a distraction for bugs while we sat outside enjoying the sounds and smells of the jungle. Two minutes after sitting down, our peace was disturbed by a very unwelcome guest. It was a flying bee or beetle the size of my fist. The buzzing sounded like a power tool. In an attempt to dissuade the insect from bothering us, we stepped inside and turned off the porch light. We assumed incorrectly that without light, the giant bug would leave. Instead, much to our terror, it began to drill through the bamboo wall with its sharp forehead protrusion. The relentless attack grew steadily louder, much like the revving of a chainsaw. We were trapped and paralyzed with fear in what had, moments earlier, seemed like a jungle paradise. With one long, low battle cry, we both stormed out of the cabin with shoes in our hands, flipping the porch light on as we ran. What ensued was a frenzy of shoe throwing, panicked running, screaming, cursing, and all-around chaos. It lasted for almost ten minutes. When it was finally over, when we had squeezed the life out of our foe, the quiet night closed in again. We gave up on peace and settled for a couple of chocolate-covered cookies and lukewarm beer, while huddling inside of our mosquito net.

Berry Crazy and the Cult Leader

Day two of our trip was rainy. I had taken my motorcycle safety class recently enough to know that it was going to be slick on the roads. I was nervous because the road between Mae Rim and Pai, our next destination, was famous for its 760 curves. It was known for being a fun ride, but when wet, very dangerous.

The road snaked its way through a series of mountain passes. Hairpin turns skirted the rocky cliffs, and the trees opened every so often to reveal magnificent views of flourishing greenery, reaching hundreds of feet to the valleys below. The damp air clung to everything around us; it was thick with the scent of soil, leaves, and the delicate white flowers perched on the branches of wild jasmine bushes.

Nathan was riding in front of me when he heard the sound of metal digging violently into pavement. My back tire hit a raised spot in the road just as I was taking a corner and slid out from under me at about twenty miles an hour. I was barely able to hold onto the bike long enough to correct away from the edge of the mountain cliff. It slid fifteen feet under me, then on top of me into the middle of the road. I quickly got myself up and moved the bike onto the shoulder. My adrenaline brought everything into sharp focus, which must be why I realized the bag of strawberries I had been carrying in the little basket attached to my handlebars had flown out during the crash. There were strawberries all over the road. Saving strawberries was instantly my top priority. I love strawberries. A vehicle could have come zipping around the corner at any minute, and my strawberries were in danger. When Nathan arrived on the scene, I was picking strawberries off the ground, laughing. I believe I asked him, "Did you *see* that? Wow. Can you help me pick up my strawberries?"

Nathan's eyes looked like they were going to fall out of his head. I giggled again, "Whoa. Your eyeballs look crazy. They're so big. It looks like your eyelids shrank."

I can't imagine what he must have been thinking. I was acting like a lunatic. I was making fun of his eyeballs. My clothes were torn, and I had blood dripping from several open wounds. I was behaving like things were perfectly normal, like I had accidentally dropped some strawberries, and stopped to pick them up. The smell of blood and burning, and the inch-deep gouges in the pavement betrayed me. He got off of his moped and walked over to make sure I was all right. My hands, which were full of strawberries and raw from road rash, were shaking. Nathan took the bloody strawberries from my clenched fingers and tossed them into the woods. He explained gently, "We're not going to eat those. Let's forget about the strawberries. We can buy more." He waited for my shaking to stop before suggesting we get back onto the bikes to find a dry place to bandage my bloodied arms and legs.

A rest stop a couple of miles down the road had shelter and warm tea. We found a spot where I could rub myself with antibiotic cream and wrap gauze around my legs and shoulder. The forty miles that remained between the accident site and the quaint mountain village of Pai took about twice as long as they should have. I was nervous to lean with my bike even on the easiest turns. The location of my bandages made us both realize that we had been seeing victims of motorcycle accidents all over the place. We hadn't put it together that all the tourist road rash we had been observing was from accidents just like mine. I had earned the badge of fatuity, like so many foreigners before me.

Pai was cheap, beautiful, and filled with people who couldn't bring themselves to leave Thailand. It was near enough to the Myanmarese border that quick visa runs were on most residents' monthly calendars. There were communes for meditation, long-term rental agreements for hillside bungalows, and pamphlets with tips on how to arrange a permanent relocation. Pai knew its own charm. It had a lively night market with vendors of all kinds, including a variety of snack options, which we hadn't seen even in Bangkok. We decided to brave the street food one evening for dinner. We walked around buying anything that looked intriguing and ate until we couldn't walk. One noteworthy morsel was a banana leaf omelet. I was so impressed with Nathan when he ordered it. The garnish was a pile of grubs, white and plump. By Nathan's expression, I realized that he had no idea what it was. I thought better of keeping it a secret. He might have abandoned me if I knowingly encouraged him to eat maggots. To his credit, he tried it anyway. So did I, but I had no qualms about throwing it into the nearest trashcan once I felt the worms popping between my teeth.

While in Pai, we took a day off from traveling together. We had been with one another almost every minute of every day for nearly three weeks. I needed time to myself. When I suggested time alone, Nathan didn't object. We had breakfast together, then headed our separate ways with a plan to meet that evening for dinner.

I did a little shopping, stuffed my face with three or four ice cream cones, and wandered the city streets. It was the first time it even occurred to me that traveling alone would be a very different experience. Without Nathan at my side, I was apparently more approachable.

I was walking thoughtfully across an unstable bamboo bridge when a gentleman stopped me. His English immediately gave him away as an American. He was in his early seventies and had a white beard that swallowed his entire face. I could barely make out his jolly grin and twinkling eyes buried beneath the mane. He made easy conversation and his laughter gave the impression that he was at peace. He said his name was Harudu. I had a guess about the origin of his tranquility, the smell of tranquility was all over the place, but I didn't let it stop me from taking the time to get to know him. I imagined Nathan in my shoes, wondered what his reaction might be to tropical Santa Claus. If he were a predator, I couldn't imagine what sort of prey would fall victim to the tools at his withering disposal. He was clearly looking for something. I smiled up at him and decided to indulge in an afternoon experiment. Maybe I would discover something unexpected.

He offered to buy me a coffee in exchange for some honest conversation. Once sipping our iced lattes, we sat in the shade, where he told me of his life as a meditation specialist. He took in wayward travelers and taught them the inner workings of their own souls. He helped them heal themselves and taught them how to love. For a man claiming the gift of emotional awareness, he was remarkably poor at gauging how unimpressed I was. Harudu was probing me, trying subtly to gather intelligence on my emotional weaknesses. He was hoping to collect another dedicated follower. Listening to him was worse than listening to a used car salesman. Even so, I couldn't bring myself to leave. I wanted to know as much as I could to satisfy my curiosity.

He pulled a book from his satchel and handed it to me. It was a book of poems that he had written and self-published. They were incomprehensible. I tried to appreciate them while he watched my eyes scan the page. He interrupted to explain the teacher–student dynamic required to study with him. Just above a whisper he said, "I ask that all of my students love me."

I looked up from my performance as an intent reader, "Hmm? What?"

"If you are going to study with me and learn to touch your own inner peace, you will need to honestly, openly, and freely love me."

"Interesting." I didn't want to derail his prepared speech. I was at full attention.

"I love you." He said with the utmost sincerity.

"Really?"

"I love that man over there." He pointed at a stranger.

"OK."

"To study with me is to love me." He finished with a strange, otherworldly smile.

I handed his book back to him, smiled in return, and wished him luck. On my way to the meeting spot that Nathan and I had picked out, I silently wished his disciples luck in extricating themselves from his love nest.

When I met up with Nathan, I couldn't put into words why I had felt the need to follow Harudu to the coffee shop or why I had listened to his story. Maybe it was because he was also an American. A fact I felt sure he used to create false bonds with distressed travelers. Harudu made a business of trolling the streets to find people in need of comfort, security, and affection. Who knows, maybe he needed those things too. I was happy to have chosen to travel with Nathan and sorry for all those backpackers wandering the villages of Southeast Asia alone, desperate for the comfort that Harudu was offering.

Nathan summed the day up succinctly, "So…you spent your day with a cult leader."

Culinary Confusion

We left Pai the next morning. It was a long ride back to Chiang Mai, but we did it in a single day. Our visas were about to expire, so we stayed one night in Chiang Mai, then took a bus north to its sister city, Chiang Rai. From there, we made a quick run to Myanmar for an extension.

On the walk from the bus station in Chiang Rai to the city center, Nathan kept stopping to sound out the words on street signs, buildings, and advertisements. It was almost four in the afternoon, we hadn't eaten lunch, and I was starving, cranky, and wanted more than anything to put down my sixty-pound pack and lie on a bed.

I finally asked, "Nathan, you don't even know what Smil-pep-hlen-gimk means, so what good does it do to sound it out? I'm slipping closer and closer to a hyperglycemic meltdown. I need food!"

This got his attention. He looked at me as if I had four heads, then answered, "Oh. Well, why haven't you eaten? I can't keep track of *your* hunger too."

I had to laugh. I had been trying to plan my mealtimes around a man, who on occasion, forgets to eat for so long that he gets headaches. Somewhere in the back of my mind I realized that I had been embarrassed that I was always the one stopping to eat. I hadn't wanted Nathan to think I was an overeater, or a stress eater. It had taken me almost a month to figure out that he wouldn't have noticed or cared, even if I were. I stopped and got some meat on a stick while he sounded out the name of the school we were passing. When he saw my food, he instantly realized his own hunger and ordered two for himself.

We took a day trip from Chiang Rai to the Union of Myanmar to deal with our visas. By leaving, and then returning to Thailand, Americans are granted a fifteen-day extension. The process is quite simple.

On our way into Myanmar, I unintentionally distracted the immigration officer, causing him to stamp Nathan into the country without asking for his entry fee. Nathan did not return the favor, so I got stuck paying the full fifteen dollars. We walked down crowded alleys, dodging the desperate pleas of children hawking cheap cigarettes and Viagra. Around midday, I started to get hungry. I didn't bother waiting for Nathan to agree to a sit-down lunch. Instead, I found a woman selling bags of delicious-looking pink dried fruit. It was something I had never seen. The fruits looked a bit like flattened breast implants with the texture of a perfectly dried apricot. They looked delicious. I tried negotiating the price and was shot down immediately. The woman selling them would take nothing less than full price. Five baht, or seventeen cents. The woman started to cut the fruit into tiny pieces, so I stopped her. I excitedly mimed that my intention was to eat it right then. I should have known something was amiss by the sly smile and head shaking, but I ate it anyway. Nathan and I walked while I snacked. Dozens of people passed, smiled knowingly at me, then the fruit, then back at me. Nathan asked, "What do you think it is that you're eating? Everyone seems far too interested."

"Oh, who knows. They probably don't see tourists eating local food very often. Maybe I'm eating it wrong."

We stayed in Myanmar for less than two hours. I felt a little guilty for not venturing more than four blocks from the border, but there were so many beggars, most of whom were children, that we couldn't bear to.

When we got to the Thailand side of the border crossing, Nathan's free pass came back to haunt him. The immigration official took one look at his passport and said, "No good." He grabbed mine, gave it a quick look and waved me through the gate. Nathan was sent back to Myanmar to sort things out. He looked over his shoulder nervously, toward Myanmar's immigration office, then back at me. I was already being herded away from him, into Thailand. He called, "Don't go far. For all I know, I might be spending the next two weeks in a prison cell."

I tried to reassure him, "It's not your fault they screwed up your passport. You're not a sneaky criminal."

"What if they think I've done something illegal?"

"I'm sure it'll be fine."

"Yes, but if it's not?"

"I'll call in the Navy Seals." I gave him a wink, then shooed him.

With that, Nathan turned and disappeared from view. I hadn't wanted to worry him by validating his concerns, but I was a little nervous too. He was at the mercy of a room full of Myanmarese border agents. I waited patiently just inside

Thailand's border. It didn't take long for Nathan to get things straightened out. Apparently, along with forgetting to collect Nathan's entry fee the immigration officer in Myanmar had stamped his passport twice, indicating that he had entered Myanmar two times in a single day without legally departing. Surprisingly, this snafu was the source of much laughter and little trouble on the Myanmar side of the crossing. We got the distinct impression that it wasn't the first time the Thai immigration officials had discovered such a mistake.

We jumped back onto a bus and returned to Chiang Rai. That evening at our hotel, my intestines began angrily churning the warning signs of a long night spent squatting. With a little investigating, I learned that the breast implant snack in Myanmar had been a local remedy for constipation. I had eaten about five hundred times the recommended dose.

Spider Bite

Our visa extensions gave us the opportunity to have one more Thai adventure. The next day, we hopped in the back of a pickup truck heading into the jungle, north of Chiang Rai. The truck dropped us off on the outskirts of an Akah Village. We walked several miles before finding a dilapidated guesthouse at the top of a hill. Tea plantations surrounded us, and the cashew trees were blooming. It was a beautiful evening, so we decided to use what light remained for another jungle walk.

We wandered to the top of a nearby hill to get a sense of our location. The land was black with soot, acres of trees and grassland, burned and cleared for cultivation. A gray haze hung just above the landscape all around us. The orderly hedges of tea plantations draped themselves across the land on both sides of the valley beyond, in a great labyrinth of geometric artistry that stretched to the horizon. We stood quietly, watching the sky slip from blue to orange in a small ring around the setting sun. For the first time in a long time, I felt stillness. I was surprised to realize that what I missed most about the United States had nothing to do with amenities like comfortable beds, grocery stores, and nights out with friends. It was the silence. It was the ability to find a quiet place, whether in nature or my own home, to breathe. I looked over at Nathan, wondering if he felt the same peace. He was attempting to extinguish several embers buried within a still-smoldering branch with a well-placed stream of urine. I went back to appreciating our surroundings. When he was finished, we slowly made our way back to the village.

At an intersection in the dirt path, we stumbled upon a man. It was hard to make out his features in the semi-darkness, but the smell of alcohol on his breath and his unsteady feet made it clear that he had been drinking. He pointed in the direction of a bamboo hut on a nearby knoll and said the words, "whiskey," "die," and "come." Then he made a motion as if to slit his own throat. We interpreted this as:

1. *Come drink whiskey or I will slit your throat.*
   Or
2. *Come drink until you die at my place.*

It would have been wrong to leave such an ambiguous invitation uninvestigated, so we did the only thing we could do. We followed the man into the darkness.

We found ourselves sitting in a circle with eight men, between the ages of thirteen and seventy, all hammered. People were laughing, eating, and drinking all around us. They welcomed us, filled our glasses to the brim with whiskey, and brought us plates of food. We tasted everything without asking any questions, but eventually our curiosity got the better of us. Most of it was pork with pieces of bone and fat that had been boiled or fried. There was only one dish I had a hard time stomaching. Soon after trying it, I learned that it was raw pork in a blood broth. I spent the remainder of the evening wishing I knew more about trichinosis.

With a little sleuthing, we discovered that we had been invited to a wedding. The throat slitting gesture was meant to convey that a pig had been slaughtered for the occasion. For the next hour, we tirelessly worked to bridge the cultural gap with whiskey. I kept sliding my full whiskey glass in front of Nathan while simultaneously sliding his empty one back toward my own place. In hindsight, this whiskey switching may have done him a service, by numbing his extremities. As the evening neared its end, I looked over to find Nathan in a state of extreme agitation. He was whacking his own inner thigh frantically. When his fit stopped, a tarantula, crumpled and broken, popped out of the leg of his shorts. Dead. In the frenzy, Nathan had scared the poor arachnid into taking a bite out of an extremely sensitive bit of skin. It's a popular myth that a tarantula bite is dangerous. It's like a bee sting, perhaps slightly more painful. Though, I thought it best to hold this observation in until long after the incident.

Nathan held up the carcass in the firelight and asked a Thai man sitting across from us if it was dangerous. "Ah…yes! Throw it into the bushes! You don't want *that* to bite you!"

Nathan anxiously and with wavering pitch, shouted, "It did *bite* me!" The man didn't seem overly concerned. He shrugged his shoulders and calmly motioned for Nathan to toss it into the dark behind a nearby hut. The Thai man noticed Nathan's incredulity at the lack of attention being paid to his suffering. He showed some token empathy by miming pain with gritted teeth, then shrugged his shoulders and offered Nathan a fresh whiskey.

We returned to Chiang Rai two days later to catch a bus to the Laos border. The road between Chiang Rai and the border crossing was paved and well cared for. It was a pleasant ride that meandered through expansive farmland and countless small villages. While appreciating the scenery, I reflected on our experiences in Thailand. Despite being unprepared at the start, we had managed to do just fine.

We had gotten to know ourselves outside of our American framework and created a home together, which traveled with us. It had been a slow transition from a lifestyle in which we derived comfort from our routines and possessions, to one in which we were comfortable in our own skins, with nothing but each other. We had successfully eased into a very close, honest, and silly relationship. One where circumstances eliminated the option for personal space and inhibitions became meaningless.

Chapter Two

Laos
Watches are for Westerners

Laos is a complex country for a Westerner, painfully so until you get the hang of it. There were a few items that should, but do not, appear on the billboard above the customs desk at all Laos border crossings.

1. Do not enter if you are on a tight schedule OR any other kind of schedule.
2. Do not enter if you are not willing to jump from the window of a moving vehicle to save your own life.

Unlike Thailand, Laos did nothing to prepare us for its unique charms. Thailand was possibly the most advanced, devious, and organized tourist trap on the planet. Its citizens worked tirelessly and cohesively to convince visitors that things were better than what they'd expected. The strategy is brilliant. Spread the word that travel in your country is amazing, but high risk. Make claims of strict law enforcement, tough regulations, and conservative behavior. Then, allow unrestricted drug and alcohol abuse, turn a blind eye to sex workers, and eliminate law enforcement from heavily trafficked tourist destinations. The result: crowds of drunk, foreign, ignoramuses, proud to have broken every rule, and gotten away with it.

In Laos, tourists do not have preconceived notions of danger or safety. Rules are not talked about, unless they have been broken. The only warning anyone receives after crossing the Mekong into Laos is about medical facilities. There *are* no medical facilities. Travelers are told not to get hurt. They are told that if they do get hurt, they will either die, or suffer terribly trying to get themselves back into Thailand for help. Most likely they will die.

Laotians are still torn between the merits of helping a tourist and the financial reward for conning one. Many find it difficult to care about preserving their country's reputation when marring that reputation means immediate and personal gain.

That said, Laos is a beautiful country. We foolishly listened to the Thai tourism department when they told us that we wouldn't need more than three or four days to explore the vast network of rivers, mountainous jungles, and isolated villages.

We crossed into Laos just before dusk on a longboat with several other tourists. Fellow travelers never cease to amaze and bewilder me. On the brief boat ride, we listened to a boy lament his misfortune. He was attempting to enter Laos for the third time in a week. He didn't have a Laotian visa and had forgotten his passport in Thailand on not one, but two previous attempts to make the crossing. His Thai visa had long ago expired, and he had just forked over most of his travel fund to pay the penalty associated with overstaying one's welcome. For someone like me, a tireless organizer and planner, his behavior was inexcusable. I didn't have much sympathy for his situation and mentioned that if he were my friend, I probably would have left him at the border. He sheepishly smiled, admitting that that was exactly what had happened. His travel partners were long gone.

Upon hearing this, I turned to Nathan and urgently whispered, "Amber alert!" The young man was the kind of vulnerable traveler that is best to avoid. If we got too close, or divulged too much of our itinerary, there was a chance he would end up mysteriously appearing for weeks because he was desperate for someone familiar.

Nathan whispered back, "Do you have a Thai child in your backpack?"

I was confused. "What? No. This backpacker is a succubus. He's looking for someone to latch onto. I was alerting you."

"You do know that amber alerts are for missing children, right?"

"This isn't America. The alert systems are totally different. Just don't get too friendly."

Nathan rolled his eyes, but followed my lead, keeping conversation short, polite, and vague. When it came time to stamp passports and make our way through customs, we were at an advantage. Our visas were ready to go, and we had exchanged some baht for kip to pay our entrance fee. We scurried away from the riverbank into the depressed town of Huay Xai.

Our first act as visitors in Laos was to drink a couple of bottles of the national beverage, Beer Laos. Our second act as visitors was inspired by our first. Nathan had, what we thought at the time, was a million-dollar idea. International Price is Right. We found a small shop with a wide variety of goods and began doing research. I would stand on one side of the store holding an item above my head. Any item. A bag of shrimp-flavored potato snacks, a small baggie full of hard candy, shampoo, or skin-whitening lotion. Nathan would search his side of the shop for an item he believed to be of equal value. We did this with great enthusiasm until the shop owner tired of trying to figure out why we were yelling at each other with tampons and Jell-O snacks held above our heads. He kicked us out of the store. We decided to buy our last two items in celebration. They had exactly the same price, one dollar. Not a bad price for a liter bottle of local whiskey, but a bit steep for a six pack of wafer cookies.

The next morning Nathan announced, "The cleanest shirt I have is covered in bat guano from a cave incident two weeks ago."

"That's the cleanest one? What's wrong with the other ones?" I asked, wondering if I wanted to know the answer. On the one hand, it was convenient that he didn't create too much laundry, but on the other, his clothes were covered in excrement.

I requested firmly that he make the time to buy another t-shirt, or two. For a man who let a thousand-dollar natural gas bill roll off of his back, Nathan was inexplicably tight with his money. He couldn't bring himself to spend six dollars for two new t-shirts.

Zip It

The only thing we planned in advance on our entire journey was in Laos. I would have planned every day, if left to my own devices, but Nathan insisted we fly by the seat of our pants. In Laos, though, there was one thing we both wanted to do badly enough that we made reservations. We wanted to visit the Bokeo Nature Reserve in northern Laos for a zip line adventure. Much of the forested land in northern Laos is vulnerable to clear cutting. China needs wood. Laos has wood, and the regional directors of land preservation in northern Laos want money. Due to corruption, the result is illegal deforestation. There are few consequences for the individuals involved, and terrible consequences for the environment and the creatures that live there. One of these creatures is the gibbon. In a bit of genius, a French man with both business sense and an environmental conscience, invented his own solution. He bought up as much of the land as he could afford to create one of the most stunning, environmentally friendly adventure parks on the planet. His tourist attraction is called The Gibbon Experience. It is a chance to live as the gibbon does, in the jungle canopy. If you're lucky, it's also a chance to observe this magically agile animal in its natural environment.

The Gibbon Experience collects two groups of eight tourists from Huay Xai each day. Participants spend either two or three nights in treehouses 150 feet in the air. By day, they travel from mountainside to mountainside, flying over valleys on a vast network of interconnected steel cables or zip lines, enjoying majestic views of the dense greenery from above.

We checked in the day before our scheduled departure to ensure our spots were saved. Huay Xai is not a tourist destination in itself; it is a transit hub with a single strip of restaurants, bars, and guesthouses all competing for the same business. We did what most people do when stuck in a town like this. We drank Beer Laos, rested in our air-conditioned room, and sampled Laotian food. The next morning, we woke early, got our things together, and headed down to The Gibbon Experience office. We watched an introductory video that was hilariously inadequate by U.S. safety standards, yet refreshingly to the point. It boiled down to: Don't be an idiot, you're several hundred feet in the air and there is no hospital in this country.

The eighteen of us who had gathered for the trip were told that two of us would have to wait for the next trip because of overbooking. Chaos ensued. For most people, this kind of news creates a sort of brain vacuum. All rational thought is sucked into a black pit of despair. Plans are ruined, buses are missed, and tight schedules are torn apart. For travelers like Nathan and I, this kind of unexpected bump in the road is simply unimportant. That said, we were *not* the two people to remain behind. A meek girl who we had eaten breakfast with that morning got stuck waiting, as did a man who showed up late. I hopped into the front seat of a truck carrying four people in the open bed and four of us inside the cab. Nathan sat behind me with a man named Enrico and a woman named Salina. As we waited for our driver, Enrico and Salina exchanged sharp words. She was incensed. From their whispered argument, I gathered that he had surprised her with this adventure, and she was deathly afraid of heights. I looked over my shoulder to make eye contact with Nathan, but his eyes were firmly planted in his own hands. Enrico was kissing every surface of Salina's red and tear-streaked face. She was shoving him away as he condescendingly guaranteed her that it would be thrilling for her to face her fears. She shook with rage and terror.

I turned back around.

I wondered if it might have been smarter to give up our places. We were stuck in a cab with an emotionally dysfunctional couple and a long ride ahead of us. Salina asked Enrico where her bag was. He told her not to worry, that it was in a pile of bags, all being transported to the site. My head snapped up. I turned back around to look at Nathan. This time his eyes were wide, like mine. We both sensed an incredibly awkward situation getting much, much worse, so I decided to speak up.

"Er, Enrico is it? I think you'd better go get your bags. They aren't being transported to the site. All of those bags in the back room are being left there by people who are taking smaller day-bags and leaving their hiking packs for three days. Whatever you need, you need to bring with you."

Salina's dangerous glare shot to Enrico. She shoved his chubby lips off her neck and called him an idiot. He was slightly slower to frenzy than she, but when he realized our driver was buckling up and he had very little time to get his things, he jumped into action screaming, "*Wait for me! I need my things!*"

He returned two minutes later, out of breath, carrying a small backpack for himself and an overstuffed pack for Salina. He tried to capitalize on the close call, hoping to smooth things over by basking in his own glory. "Wow, that was almost a disaster. Good thing I got our bags!" Salina rolled her eyes and got as far away from him as possible, which meant getting closer to Nathan.

I wish our time with Salina and Enrico had ended with that truck ride, but when we reached our destination, try as we might, we couldn't get ourselves in a group that did not contain them. We were forced to make the journey through the Bokeo Nature Reserve in the company of this duo. Our trek began with a five-minute walk followed by a twenty-minute lunch break. We sat by the bank of a creek eating our banana leaf-wrapped sandwiches while we all introduced ourselves. There was Alina, a straight-shooting German girl, with the pluck to travel alone through Southeast Asia. Then there was Lora, a fiery redhead traveling with her girlfriend Maud. They were both from Holland and close to the end of their six months of backpacking. A fellow American named Rachel was on the trip, close to the end of her travels as well. Lastly Enrico, an alleged Spanish writer living in Bangkok, and his fiancé Salina, a Filipino tornado. We were accompanied by two guides, both of whom spoke rudimentary English.

We walked single file, chatting with the travelers nearest to us. Nathan and I instantly felt comfortable with everyone, and had a great time sharing stories and getting to know one another. Enrico and Salina hung behind, arguing, and in her case, crying.

The real adventure began in the middle of the afternoon when we reached the first zip line. Our harnesses were all waiting for us at a campsite. We were shown with a twenty-second demonstration how to put them on, then how to hook them to the steel cable wound around a gigantic tree on the mountainside. The braking system was elegantly simple. To stop, we had to squeeze an old bicycle tire around the cable. The tires were attached to our harnesses at our waists with rope and a carabiner. Our guide could hardly contain his own excitement. He was already perched on the wooden platform where the cable met the tree, ready to demonstrate. He attached his clip to the thick cable extending out above the jungle and waited for everyone's attention. The line ran over a quarter of a mile to a tree on the slope of a mountainside across the valley from us. With a wave and giggle, our guide pushed himself off of the platform and zipped into the open air. It was exhilarating just to watch. We all lined up with anticipation. Lora jumped up onto the platform and screamed, *"Clear?"* From the other side of the valley came our guide's voice, *"Clear."* She hooked her old tire around the cable, leaned back, held her safety line tight, and was off. Each one of us in turn hooked our harnesses and brakes to the line and flew into the air with a yelp.

Salina was the last of us to step onto the platform. The second guide had remained behind to ensure that everyone made it safely across the valley. I can only imagine what that poor man must have had to do to get Salina to clip-in, and zip across a line that dangled about 300 feet in the air. She was terrified and sobbing hysterically. She made it within twenty feet of the finishing platform. We all tried to tell her to use her brake, but fear paralyzed her. She started screaming for help as she slowly slid back, all the way to the low spot at the center of the line. She hung, body shaking, hands gripping the ropes at her waist, suspended above the jungle. She was panic-stricken. I hadn't felt much empathy for her until that moment. Her jerk-face fiancé, who knew she was afraid of heights, had surprised her with the worst trip she could have possibly imagined. To top it off, she was suffering this fate while nine people stared in disbelief. Thankfully, our guide didn't seem concerned. He clipped back in and carefully slid down to the middle of the line to grab her. He calmed her down, snatched her harness, and dragged her painstakingly back to the finishing platform. Her back was nearly bent in half with the weight of her pack and her tiny arms were shaking from the exertion of having to hold herself upright. When her feet were on solid ground, she gathered herself. Nine expectant faces watched as she deliberately lifted her head and met Enrico's gaze. He had an obnoxious grin on his face. "You did it, Babe! I'm so proud of you."

Her expression darkened. "I hate you Enrico." She turned to the guide. "I will not be doing another zip line. I'm done. Take me home."

At this point, everyone but Enrico, Salina, and the guide began to move away from the scene. We all knew the answer to Salina's demand. Impossible. We had been briefed that the first zip line took all trekkers into the jungle without a hiking trail back. The only way out was to zip out. Salina was going to have to zip at least twelve more times over the next three days, before she would be able to go home.

We ended our first day in a picturesque treehouse with breathtaking views in every direction. Our guide waited for all of us to arrive safely, remove our harnesses, and drop our bags. He gave a brief treehouse tour, promised to send food, then zipped back into the jungle, wishing us a good night's sleep. Our beds were thin mattresses spread around the treehouse, each with a sheet hung above it for privacy. The bathroom was a floor below us, open to the jungle. To reach it, we had to lift a hatch in the floor and make our way down thin steps while clinging to rafters and walls for support. There were thousands of holes drilled into the floorboards below a rusty shower nozzle. It was obvious they were meant for drainage, but none of us felt comfortable standing on a section of floor that had been so compromised. Lora took the initiative to move the nozzle to a more structurally sound location. The bathroom walls were open, though enclosed by a double railing at stomach height. Standing naked in the crisp evening air, while gazing out at the fading blue sky, was surprisingly luxurious. It felt liberating to bear all in such an exposed, elevated place, yet safe at the same time. Each of us in turn washed the grime from our skin and hair while the others waited above. The water was tepid and the pressure low, but we were all grateful to have it. Besides the shower, water was also piped into the kitchen sink, which sat bolted to the trunk at the center of the shelter. Near the sink hung a small solar-powered lamp.

Earlier that day, each of us had purchased a bottle of Beer Laos from a man sitting in his rice field. We cracked our bottles and waited for the sound of our dinner arriving.

Not long after we had all cleaned up and found seats near a makeshift wooden table, we heard the telltale humming of the cable. The sound of metal sliding on metal changed pitch as it grew closer, finally ending in a high whine as a man carrying five containers full of food was hurled into our midst. He hadn't had a free hand to apply the brake to his line, so had arrived at full speed. We asked him to stay and enjoy our meal with us, but he declined with a bow. He ran to the return cable, clipped himself in, and jumped headfirst from the side of the treehouse. His gleeful squeals echoed in the darkness as he disappeared, sliding gracefully through the jungle. The eight of us spent the evening chatting, playing cards and laughing. Even Salina was able to forget her discomfort for a few minutes while telling us of her home. Six of us made plans to rise early the next morning, to zip a few times before our guides returned to take us to the next treehouse.

That night we were awakened by terrifying cracks of thunder. The lightning was very close, and the tree swayed with the wind and the rain. Our privacy sheet kept us dry while we peeked out into the night. Lying with Nathan in the warm, protected cocoon of our jungle treehouse, I felt at home. Even though Nathan was powerless to protect me from death by fiery inferno if lightning struck, I felt safe and perfectly content.

The next morning, everyone but Enrico and Salina woke early. By the time the first light was creeping through the branches above us, we were all strapped into our harnesses ready to move. We had three hours to explore the lines before we were picked up by our guide for the next leg of the journey.

Alina led the way. The line exiting our treehouse was different from the other lines we had been on. All previous ones had gently lifted from the slope of a mountain, easing us into the sky. This line began over 150 feet in the air, suspended from the trunk of a tree. There was nothing gentle about the way we had to fling ourselves into the open. We each held on to the hope that our carabiners were new and our ropes were strong.

The thick metal cable that left our shelter disappeared into the morning fog. We couldn't make out the platform on the other end of the line, or even the trees on the other side of the valley we were zipping across. As each of us jumped in turn, our bodies became hazy to those behind, then disappeared altogether. The sound of our carabiners against the cables and the slight swaying of the lines were the only indication that someone was on the move. After we all reached the platform on the other end of the cable and climbed down, we realized we had neglected to ask our guide how to finish the loop. Zip lines are one-way. We walked through the woods on a worn path, not knowing if we were heading in the right direction. Eventually, we came to another platform on a mountain ridge, with a cable extending from the ancient tree supporting it. The fog had become a white blanket around us. There was no telling how long, or how high the cable was, or where it ended. We had no way of knowing if we would be stranded without our bags, or our guides. If I had been alone,

I would never have chosen to take the risk. Nathan, on the other hand, had no qualms about throwing caution to the wind. He clipped in, gave a mischievous grin, and threw himself from the platform.

His line hummed for what seemed like forever. After the first five seconds of his flight, he became invisible to us all. We waited, holding our breath for the sounds of his demise. When no sound came, the others all looked to me, as if to apologize for not stopping him. I couldn't very well leave him stranded, so I followed.

The line seemed to stretch for miles. It was the longest yet. I knew that each trip lasted no more than forty-five seconds, but time wasn't the same while zipping through fog. I had no way of knowing how far I had gone, or how far there was to go. I could see the cable ten feet to either side of my own body, but no further. I was floating in a cloud, untouchable. Unexpectedly, I heard the hissing of an approaching carabiner. I started to tense at the idea of a head-on collision with Nathan. What was he thinking? How could he be coming back on the same line? It was impossible. Even so, the metallic hum grew louder, then I heard Nathan's screaming hoots and felt them pushing through the thick air toward me.

It was dumb luck that I saw him pass below me. I happened to be glancing down at the exact moment his body, arms and legs splayed, flew past my own, not twenty feet from my dangling limbs. He had managed to find the return cable and clip-in, just as I was leaving the opposite slope. The others were excited to try the same maneuver. We spent almost three hours crossing the valley in one direction, hiking up a steep slope, then crossing back in the other. When our legs were tired of climbing the same mountain trail over and over, we headed back to collect Salina and Enrico.

We were all pleasantly surprised by the level of freedom our guides gave us. We followed them through the maze of trails, but for the most part, they gave us time to enjoy the lines without the pressure of a schedule. Salina and Enrico continued to be outrageously incompatible. I couldn't imagine them having anything but a long and painful future together. They both found themselves in the group's collective doghouse because of their ridiculous behavior.

On the morning of our second day, some of us zipped back to the treehouse for water, to find Salina sitting cross legged, writing in her journal, on Lora's bed. Her mud caked boots rested on the pillow.

Enrico managed to infuriate everyone by using an entire roll of toilet paper in one, painfully audible, bathroom visit. We felt for him, but his generous paper usage left the rest of us without, for the remainder of the trip.

Despite sharing the journey with a couple of buffoons, we loved every minute of The Gibbon Experience. We weren't lucky enough to see any gibbons swinging through the trees, but we did hear them calling to one another in the distance.

The Slow Boat

The original plan had been to finish The Gibbon Experience then move straight to Vietnam, but after our trip to the Bokeo Nature Reserve, we couldn't bring ourselves to leave without seeing more of the Laotian countryside. We returned reluctantly to Huay Xai to find transportation south. Some of our new friends, Alina and Rachel, were heading south by bus. Lora and Maud were taking the slow boat. We had heard stories about the slow boat. It took two days of floating down the Mekong in an overcrowded, painfully slow, and dangerously constructed river craft in the sweltering heat. I thought a bus sounded much safer, and more comfortable.

The six of us met for dinner the night before our mass exodus from Huay Xai, to say goodbye. We neglected to mention the rendezvous to Salina and Enrico.

Later that night, when we had said our goodbyes, Nathan convinced me that I should loosen up about the slow boat. He assured me that taking it was something that all backpackers had to do, even if it they knew it was going to be miserable. So, I reluctantly agreed.

Our final destination was Luang Prabang, the most romantic city in Southeast Asia, so we had been told. We were informed by our hotel receptionist in Huay Xai, who sold us our slow boat tickets, that the boat left at nine the next morning. Our tickets had the numbers four and five on them. He said that they were seats right at the front of the boat and that we would be happy with them. He was right. We were happy with our seats, but not because of the numbers on our tickets. It was because the boat left at twelve thirty in the afternoon, not nine in the morning. No matter what country you're in, arriving somewhere four hours early usually guarantees you get the seat you want. None of the seats had numbers on them. They were lawn chairs, which weren't attached to the deck or each other. Nonetheless, Nathan referred to our seats as four and five for the duration of the journey, even though we were about nine rows from the front.

Slow boats were probably designed to carry about sixty people. In the United States, a boat like this would have a maximum capacity of fifty if it could pass a safety inspection, which I am certain it couldn't. In Laos, there is no such thing as maximum capacity.

When our boat was nearly finished loading, a man stood up at the front and explained in broken English that we were waiting for a tour group with eighty people, which would be arriving from northern Laos. Everyone on the boat laughed, until we realized it wasn't a joke. When the group arrived, they started cramming into the boat. There weren't nearly enough seats for all of them, so one man asked the captain, "When this boat is full, where do we go? Is there a second boat?" The captain chuckled heartily and replied, "One boat only."

Those poor travelers that couldn't or wouldn't cram themselves into a dangerously overloaded vessel, were forced to linger another day in Huay Xai. In my opinion, four hours early was worth our seats.

    We had been in Laos long enough to grasp some of its unique qualities. To call it a laid-back country wouldn't do it justice. This was a place where timing was *not* everything. If it happened, it happened. Most plans were irrelevant. While we sat in our lawn chairs, Nathan eavesdropped on a British woman ranting about Huay Xai. She compared it to a black hole. She had been trying to get out of town on a bus for three days, but every time she showed up to catch it, something came up. The driver was sick. The tires were flat. Gas was too expensive. Every day there was a new reason for a delay in departure. The woman was frantic. Her eyes were bloodshot, and a vein in her throat was pumping globs of thick blood from her wobbly head. Nathan couldn't control his giggles. He took such joy in this poor woman's frustration. In Laos, he had the opportunity to watch the kinds of people that had been scolding and belittling him his entire life, for his lack of planning and chronic lateness, squirm and suffer at the hands of a culture that suited *him* so nicely. People like me. He was overjoyed that a place so perfect for him existed and was so effectively the bane of anal-retentive people's existence. I didn't necessarily think her story was funny. I could empathize with her frustration and almost believed her accusations that the locals had her trapped, in a conspiracy to bleed money from her bank account. Nathan was tickled pink by a breathy description of her great escape (the slow boat). He admitted that the Laotian disregard for deadlines and schedules validated his own sense of timing.

    The slow boat took two days, as expected. The first night, everyone disembarked at a little town called Pakbeng. It had plenty of hotel rooms, restaurants, drug dealers, and bars to accommodate the mob of tourists that arrived every day between three and five.

    We found a place to stay, ate a hefty dinner, then went to bed. The next morning, we made sure to find our seats early for another long ride.

At the end of the second day, the slow boat dropped us at the bottom of a fifty-foot staircase that climbed crookedly to the charming streets of Luang Prabang. The city's cobblestone streets meandered through French-influenced architecture. There were street markets, music, and hundreds of milkshake vendors, all quaintly packed into the narrow peninsula. I insisted that we stay for at least a few days, to take advantage of chocolate-Oreo-coffee-mango shakes, if nothing else. We had been traveling for almost a month and a half and I was ready to stay in one place for more than two days. It was probably this craving for some semblance of stability that got me thinking about the future. I daydreamed about life back in the States. I wondered aloud what Nathan and I would do when we returned, where we might live (together), and what kind of work we would look for. It didn't occur to me that this is one of those things that scares the crap out of most men. A new girlfriend planning for something anywhere between one and ninety years in the future, like it's no big deal. In my defense, even if my plans never work out, I feel better having them. I can live with being wrong. It's much harder to live without any expectations at all.

I should have realized that while traveling, Nathan would resist my attempts to plan for the future. I got the feeling he took great pleasure in exposing me to what he called, "the benefits," of living in the moment. For the most part, I considered the results of living in the moment to be consequences, not benefits. Despite our opposite viewpoints, I held out hope that Nathan would eventually see the infinite wisdom in having a solid plan.

It was only six weeks into our trip, so I tabled talk about the future and went back to discussing issues like how the wart on his hand had miraculously disappeared since he had started taking care of his lucky mole hair.

Indigo and Excrement

We spent our days exploring Buddhist temples and street markets in Luang Prabang. One bright morning as we sipped our terrible cups of Nescafe coffee-flavored water, Nathan asked, "Do you ever wake up in the morning having no idea where you are? I do. Every morning."

It had started happening to me too. We changed hotels so frequently that the night before when I had woken up to use the bathroom, I stepped out of bed and walked face-first into a wall. It was hard to keep track of the layout of our rooms when they changed almost every night. Thankfully, Nathan hadn't woken up for this incident, even though I landed hard on the linoleum floor at the foot of the bed.

"That's just silly. I always know where I am." I answered coolly.

We heard from another guest at our hotel about a community just across the Nam Ou River that made paper and silk. Having nothing else planned, we made our way to the river crossing. A rickety bamboo bridge was suspended about twenty-five feet above the rippling water. The water couldn't have been more than two feet deep in most spots. The crossing could have easily been done on foot. A troll of a man sat on the near bank, where the bridge met the soil. He asked us for two thousand kip to make the crossing. Twenty-five cents seemed a fair price for the chance to cross a bridge with a door. The door was cut from a panel of aluminum roofing and propped in the center of the structure. It hung open but looked to be capable of locking. I could not imagine why this door seemed necessary to the locals.

Ahead of us, a monk was crossing the bridge. He stopped about halfway and sat down, legs dangling lifelessly, forlorn expression melting his features into old age. We passed him on our way to the far bank and gave a nod. I was careful not to bump him, as contact with a woman is strictly forbidden.

Below him, the water was shallow; there were rocks jutting precariously from its surface. I whispered to Nathan, "I hope he doesn't do something crazy." Then, he jumped. More accurately, he let himself fall face-first into the river. He floated to the surface about ten feet downstream. We watched in horror, as the current carried him another twenty feet. He lay motionless in the muddy water. I turned to Nathan with a worried frown. I hadn't planned on monk CPR and wasn't entirely sure I wouldn't get arrested for sucking one's face. With perfect timing, the wily trickster popped out of the water and looked up at us. His face appeared thirty years younger as it contorted with loud guffaws. I shook my head in disbelief and gave the man the smile he had been waiting for. He was clearly an expert. We had been tricked by a Deadmonk's Float.

We found the small village we had been looking for about fifteen minutes later. It was midday and the sun was blazing; we were dripping with sweat. The temperature was hovering above 100 degrees and our sun block was melting off our skin. The village was deserted. No one but a fool would be out walking in the afternoon sun. The locals were all holed up in their homes trying to keep cool. We were able to explore paper-making shops and silk weaving facilities without a single interruption. There was a slight possibility that our exploration was actually trespassing, but we couldn't be sure.

I found a vat of dye for the silk being woven at one facility and couldn't help myself. I had to stick my fingers into the unsupervised indigo liquid to see just how bright the color was. Apparently, manure is an ingredient in these all-natural dyes. The slight disturbance my fingers made in the surface of the liquid somehow aerosolized the stench of three-week-old cow dung. Nathan was not impressed. Neither was I when I realized the nearest soap was at least a mile away. I smelled like feces for the rest of the afternoon. Nathan kept close track of which hand he held and which items I touched with the offending fingers.

Once I had gotten myself cleaned up enough to stop Nathan's gagging, we decided on another street-food dinner. In Thailand, the food was, for the most part, recognizable (minus Chinatown). In Laos, there were many items being sold in dark alleys that I had never seen before, and could not, if my life depended on it, have figured out their main ingredients. Having recently eaten maggots and questionable meats on sticks, I opted for more desserts than entrees. We discovered that many of the Laotian desserts contained mungbean. I grew up on a bean farm, so naturally have a healthy respect for the bean. Even so, I would have never, in 100 years, bet that a bean could make the tastiest dessert in all of Laos. If you mash a mungbean into a fine paste, cover it in a gooey rice batter, then dip it in coconut sugar, you end up in heaven. We also discovered a tapioca gelatin square covered in coconut and freshly squeezed sugar cane juice. When we'd had our fill of sugary treats, we took a break from eating sweets to try some of the best beef jerky I have ever had. I use the word *beef*, but in reality, that is a guess wildly unsupported by hard evidence. Whatever it was, it was delicious.

Sharing is Caring

Our extended stay in Luang Prabang gave me time to reflect. I had been observing Nathan's behavioral patterns for almost two months. I was discouraged to learn that his toothbrush-sharing habit was the tip of the iceberg. He regularly invaded my boundaries by eating my snacks, drinking my water, using my things, and once, though not on purpose, wearing my clothes. My suspicions that Nathan was a Communist sympathizer were confirmed when he finally decided to buy a new t-shirt. It quickly became his prized possession. A giant hammer and sickle was printed in red, on the front. Nathan is the kind of person that made Communists believe Communism was possible. He has no real sense of ownership, works hard at whatever he does, and feels that community and common purpose build societies. He is as willing to give up the things he has as he is willing to take things from others.

I too am a firm believer in community, working hard, and sharing, but only to a point. I also like being able to keep what I've earned. I tried to explain this over dinner one night. I asked some pointed questions about Nathan's childhood to discover the origin of his ownership-understanding. His poor younger brother had constantly battled his communal property mentality. Nathan assumed that if his brother wasn't using something, like a snowboard or a pair of pants, that the item was up for grabs. According to Nathan, eventually the person he borrowed from would want something of his in return and take it. To Nathan, this was sharing.

I grew up in a house with three brothers, so most of my things were not in danger of being borrowed by my siblings, but those things that were, I strictly guarded. I like to share. For me, however, the word *share* implies foreknowledge of the arrangement.

When I asked Nathan what happened when one person didn't want anything from the people around them, he waved a hand dismissively, "Unlikely."

I was preparing to launch into a rant about personal property and individual rights when I noticed the smirk growing on his face. He was getting too good at pushing my buttons.

I scolded lightly, "You might think you're joking with me, but you still have some of that sharing is stealing mentality left over from your childhood."

He lifted his eyebrows in mock surprise. "What? I've come a long way…" His words were cut short by a guttural moan as he took the first bite of *my* chocolate mousse. Not just a bite, the first bite. I had to laugh.

"Yes, what a long way you've come. It's hard to believe how much progress."

He nodded vigorously, savoring my dessert.

Before leaving Luang Prabang, I splurged and bought Nathan a watch made out of cotton, for fifty cents. The hour and minute hands were sewn at angles never seen on an actual time telling device. It was the perfect gift to celebrate his commonality with the people of Laos. I told him that we would need to be getting up early to catch our eight-hour boat north on the Nam Ou River. He looked at his new watch and said, "Sure, I'll set my alarm."

When the Money Runs Out

The Nam Ou River wound its way through cliffs and jagged mountains for miles and miles, into the wilderness. We were going to a place where banks, currency exchanges, and often electricity, were impossible to find. This meant making sure we had enough money to find our way back to civilization once we had finished exploring. The kip is like monopoly money. If you're in Laos playing the game, it's great, and the more you have, the better. If you leave Laos with kip, it's like handing a bank teller wizard dollars and expecting a deposit slip. No one will exchange the kip for other currency. If you leave Laos with kip, the joke is on you. There were three cities in Laos that had ATMs. Luang Prabang was one of them. Trying to decide how much kip to take with us was tricky. We needed enough to get us into Vietnam, but not so much that we would arrive with a pocket full of expensive tinder. We decided on two million kip, about 120 dollars, each.

The next morning, we boarded a tiny boat with ten other travelers. Our destination was a small town called Nong Kiew. The ride was scenic and peaceful, though a bit tough in some places due to low water levels. We were traveling in the middle of the dry season. At one point, the captain turned to his passengers and said, "OK. Now you get out to push." Everyone hopped into the shallow water, and with the help of some local children, pushed the boat over a rocky patch. Without Nathan's approval, I donated half of our afternoon snack stockpile to the five children who'd helped. Watching their reaction, you would have thought I handed over a pile of gold.

We broke down twice. The first time was a minor problem. The engine was running low on oil, spitting plumes of black smoke. It took thirty minutes of deliberation for our captain to agree with his wife's opinion that he must add oil. The second breakdown had us stranded on the shore of a gold mining town for over three hours. I tried my hand at panning with little success. I did manage to bridge the cultural gap by providing the material for a middle-aged woman's comedy routine. She had a group of her panning friends rolling on the ground with laughter as she imitated my every move in a solo performance that culminated in a ridiculous battle between a shovel-wielding monkey (presumably me) and a pile of dirt. I took the hint and left the hunt for gold to the locals.

The trip taught me an essential lesson about boat travel. It is vital to choose the proper attire. As a woman, the ability to squat and pee at any moment must be a top priority. The eight-hour boat ride took twelve, and bathroom stops were not scheduled. If you had to pee, or worse, you had to ask the captain to pull to the side of the river and let you hop out. Most of the time it was an open beach, or rocky expanse of impossibly exposed land.

I learned the tricks of the trade from watching the captain's wife, who sat with him at the front of the boat and ate rice for eleven hours. She would jump off the boat whenever she could, to squat in her skirt. Often, she was no more than four feet from her husband's passengers. I could hear her pee hitting rocks beneath her, yet I saw nothing. She was a stealthy and experienced public urinator.

We made it to Nong Kiew by nightfall. It was a stunning riverside town surrounded by jungle cliffs. We found a little bungalow overlooking the river and dropped our bags. We were both starving, thanks to my generosity. We sat on our balcony after dinner, swinging in our hammocks, daydreaming about what adventures we might try in such a lovely and desolate region.

The next morning, our daydreams were shattered when we realized how much things cost in lovely, desolate regions of Laos.

A lot. We were also both surprised to learn that somehow my wallet contained about half of what we had agreed to bring, and Nathan's contained a quarter. He tried convincing me that he had been pulling more than half of his share for the last couple of days, but I was skeptical. Either way, we were cutting it close. We had just enough money to spend one more night, then catch a bus to the only town within hundreds of miles with an ATM. Oudom Xai. Nathan was hesitant about going there because he said the name made it sound like the capital city of an empire of evil Orcs, but we didn't have a choice.

We didn't waste our brief time in Nong Kiew. The landscape was different from anything I had ever seen, with giant limestone karsts obtruding from the horizon. I don't remember exactly how we heard about the caves, but we decided to brave the afternoon sun, yet again. We walked a mile and a half slathered in sunblock.

The caves were high above the valley floor. They had a narrow, rusted staircase winding to their mouth. Kids waited at the base of the staircase with dozens of flashlights for rent. Each light was equipped with a bulb that put out the tiniest fraction of a watt. This ensured that each visitor would also need a guide, which proved to be a profitable business opportunity for local children. I couldn't say no to the four-year-old Laotian boy speaking broken English, trotting behind me, wearing a pair of hand-me-down Nikes. A little girl grabbed Nathan's hand and the little boy latched onto mine. They dragged us up into the cave with much ado. "Be careful!", "Watch your step!", "Wet rocks!" They practiced their English phrases on us with little smiles and shined their own flashlights at our feet to keep us from tripping. The cave was immense. It had been the secret hiding place of Laotian military forces trying to avoid detection by American planes, as they destroyed the Ho Chi Min trail. Nathan carried our only effective flashlight, one of our own headlamps. Instead of using it to light the path, he started shining it above his own head, dragging his little tour guide much faster than mine could move. I found myself in near darkness with the little boy. He kept me at a painfully slow pace and held my hand firmly to keep me balanced. Just before I stepped into a three-foot crag in the rock, he yelled for me to stop while pointing at my near miss.

I daydreamed about ending things with Nathan to free up some time to pursue adopting a Laotian son as we worked to catch up.

Caves were a wonderful thing in Southeast Asia. Sometimes we were guided by innocent children looking for tips, other times we were on our own. In the United States, we would have had to sign death waivers for most of the caves we explored. Our American guides would have been certified spelunkers and EMTs, not first graders.

Our child guides offered their flashlights as they waved us forward. They were probably forbidden from going beyond a certain point in the maze of dark passages. We left them and continued downward, using a rotting bamboo ladder propped against the rock. Eventually, we found our way to a gash in the side of the mountain that let light from the afternoon sun into the cavity where we stood. From below, we could see the little boy sitting at the top of the ladder. He began to sing. It was the eeriest thing I have ever heard. The echo of his little voice could have been the legitimate start to any horror film. It was terrifying and beautiful.

He waited for us to finish exploring, then walked us back to the small table to return our lights. I didn't wait for him to ask for a tip. Instead, I took several thousand kip from my pocket and handed it to him. His grin went ear to ear, and he shared his final English phrase, "Thank you, Miss."

Nathan offered a tip to his guide as well, and the two children skipped off together, giggling with pride.

Our time in Nong Kiew was short, but lovely. We spent our last evening relaxing in our riverside bungalow. We weren't sure what we would do in Oudom Xai, but thought it best we schedule in some time for financial planning. While Nathan napped on our balcony hammock, I used my free time to wash my hair for the first time in two weeks. We had bathed in rivers and waterfalls, but that kind of clean wasn't quite the same as a shower. Washing in freshwater streams came with a price. In my case, a fungal one. I discovered an angry patch of ringworm while getting to know my neon pink hotel soap. I considered keeping it a secret from Nathan. I was worried it might disrupt the good thing we had going. Unfortunately, he noticed my uncomfortable itching later that evening. The honeymoon was officially over. When your boyfriend helps you put anti-fungal cream on your ringworm rash, you've taken things to the next level whether you wanted to or not.

Soggy

We left early the next morning on an ancient bus for Oudom Xai. It had been raining all night and the road leaving Nong Kiew was rough, really rough. When we were satisfied that the man standing on the top of the bus had tied our bags down tightly enough, we found our seats. Our driver walked the center aisle front to back and offered each passenger a plastic bag. When we gave him a confused look, he mimed throwing up into it. Apparently, Laotians don't travel well. It was at that exact moment that the man behind me started simultaneously burping and dry heaving. The bus hadn't even started to move. I pointed a finger over my shoulder to indicate there were others with a more pressing need.

During the ride, we narrowly missed spectacular head-on collisions (twice) with dump trucks, and we were forced to listen to the bus horn around every corner, of which there were many. I fully supported the relentless honking of horns as our bus careened down single-lane mountain roads, tipping slightly at the hairpins and slowing down for nothing. Apart from the terror, the stunningly beautiful ride was enjoyable. Dense fog from the mountain tops slid down every peak and ridge into the valleys below, alive with slow determination to escape the biting cold. These white slug clouds faded where they touched the green jungle flora, but more followed in their wake.

Oudom Xai is not a town worth visiting unless you too, find yourself low on cash and desperate. The food was not remarkable, the lodging moldy, and the people slightly grumpier than usual. We collected our cash and continued to Phongsaly on the next available bus. The rain never ceased, and the road conditions continued to worsen as we headed north, farther into the mountains of middle-of-nowhere Laos. Only once in my life have I been more terrified in a vehicle. One of my older brother's ex-girlfriends had a sociopath for a mother. She tried to kill me in her 1971 minivan by *"accidentally dozing off"* while driving over a one-lane bridge, suspended above a 300-foot ravine. The ride to Phongsaly paralleled that terror. We drove hundreds of feet above a gorge. The road, to the best of my knowledge, was made of mud. Landslides were not uncommon because there were no trees on the slope, and the muddy track was not protected by guard rails. I opened my window to prepare for the inevitable. I was certain the bus was moments from losing control. When it did, I intended to throw myself from it. I was prepared to do almost anything to save my own life, rather than remain in my seat as the bus slipped from the side of the mountain into the abyss below.

We were freezing even with the windows closed, but when Nathan saw my panicked eyes and heard me explain why our window was open, he nodded his approval.

"I don't think we're both going to make it out of this window." He said with a frown. "Promise to tell everyone that I died saving your life."

I promised.

Instead of dying miserable deaths, we arrived in Phongsaly after dark, dreading the process of finding a hotel. It was pouring rain and the air had gotten significantly colder. I wasn't sure we were any better off than we would have been lying in a mucky ditch at a lower altitude, because at least there, it would have been warmer. Phongsaly is the highest town in Laos, sitting over a mile above sea level. We had been told that it was one of the most spectacularly scenic places in the country.

The bus station was two miles out of town. This was one of my greatest gripes about Southeast Asian transport. My theory was that towns built their transport stations as far away from everything important as they could. In my opinion, they did it to drum up business for local taxi drivers, tuk tuks, and moped taxis. It also allowed these drivers to charge whatever they wanted. Ten dollars for a three-mile ride on the back of some guy's moped might seem worth it if you have a pack that weighs fifty pounds and it's thirty degrees. At least, to most normal people it might. I can't say how many times Nathan and I refused to be bamboozled and walked miles with our packs out of spite. This was not one such occasion. It was dark, wet, the temperature had fallen below forty degrees, and we were exhausted. We quickly lugged our packs into a tuk tuk and prepared to hand over whatever price was demanded.

On the wet ride to town, we noticed the husband and wife pair we had seen at a restaurant in Oudom Xai, the night before. Their names were Ben and Deb. They were the friendliest faces we had seen in a long time. They offered us some advice from their travel book about places to stay in Phongsaly. The conversation helped distract us from the miserable ride. We all sat huddling and shivering in the back of the tuk tuk, which did little to protect us from the driving rain. We were dropped off at the top of a hill in the center of town. Everyone scattered in search of a warm, dry place. We took the first room we found. Ben and Deb had located the guesthouse before us and were on their way out, to look for a meal. They wished us luck as they darted into the rain.

The beds were essentially wooden benches. There was no heat, no electricity, and only a single ratty blanket for us to share. The temperature had plummeted even further, hovering just above freezing. Our extremities were bloodless. To top off the discomfort, we were hungry. I suggested crawling into our bed until it was time to leave Phongsaly, but Nathan insisted that we eat something. With much grumbling, he pulled me from our room to wander the streets of a town we had never seen a map of, in the rain. After walking for twenty minutes through mucky streets, we found a hotel that had a restaurant sign inside. We entered. Much to our surprise, we found Ben and Deb, who'd just finished a meal. They informed us that the woman in the back would cook fried rice for us, but only rice because that's all she had. We sat down in a barren ballroom at the only table in the facility. We could hear the echo of our voices coupled with the occasional clanking of a pan or utensil. I ignored the intel about fried rice and ordered noodle soup. Our waitress said OK, then asked Nathan what he wanted. He tried for some fried rice and was told that the only thing she had was noodle soup. Most likely, she didn't want to prepare two different meals, so the only thing she *had* was the thing the first person ordered. Two noodle soups it was.

Phongsaly didn't get better, it got worse. It rained for three days straight and was so cold we stayed wrapped up in blankets the whole time. The rain clouds and fog reduced our visibility to a few feet, and without the scenic views, Phongsaly had little going for it.

The road out of town was blocked by a landslide and was almost impassable. Almost. I explained calmly to Nathan the morning of our intended departure that he should be prepared for the worst-case scenario. I fully intended to walk the twelve miles to Muang Houng, schlepping my pack, if need be. Nothing could have stopped me from extricating myself from the misery. It was a shame we never got to see what all the postcards and travel books raved about, but I was finished with attempting to wait out the weather. I had run out of clean socks to wear as mittens, and no matter how many tank tops I tied together and wrapped around my neck, I was borderline hypothermic.

We walked to the bus stop on the other side of town, meeting up with Ben and Deb en route. They had been stranded in their dank hotel room for three days as well. I think Deb was both impressed by my ingenuity, and embarrassed to be seen speaking to a girl wearing her boyfriend's tube socks as earmuffs. Several locals loaded a bag, dripping blood, onto the top of the bus with the rest of the bags. It likely contained the chopped up remains of a cow. At least, that's what I hoped.

We bounced along on an uneven, mud-slicked road while blood dripped eerily down the window of the seat in front of us. The bus stopped in the middle of nowhere, at which point the driver announced that he would go no further. There was a landslide ahead. He promised that he would call a tuk tuk driver from the town on the other side, to give us a ride, if we walked to meet him. The locals seemed OK with this proposition, so we followed suit. All of our things were unloaded and we started walking. Eventually, we made it to the tuk tuk, which delivered us to the boat landing in Muang Houng. There, we found a boat to carry us downriver to a small town called Muang Khua. Buses departed every other day from Muang Khua to the Vietnamese border.

International Bank of Idiots

We arrived in Muang Khua with millions of kip in our pockets, exactly what we had been trying to avoid. We had taken out far too much money in Oudom Xai and were dangerously close to leaving Laos with piles of useless currency. Ben and Deb started helping us to advertise ourselves as a currency exchange. By that evening, we had unloaded most of our money to travelers arriving from Vietnam. We set up our exchange counter at a bar, right next to the unloading dock, and did our best to lure in travelers with extra dong, (Yes, Vietnam's currency is *really* called dong). Ben and Deb joined us for drinks and dinner, and we finally took the time to get to know them. Ben was a jolly man. He was a younger and non-creepy version of Harudu. He had a big white beard, friendly smile, and an easy laugh. Deb had a way of making us feel like guests, which I found miraculous and comforting at the same time. What I liked best about Ben and Deb was how obvious it was that they loved each other. I found myself wishing that someday Nathan and I would travel again and be like them. They were from Canada, both nearing retirement. They had traveled in Southeast Asia before, and were back to visit some of their favorite places. It turned out that our paths would likely cross several more times, as they were heading in the same direction.

The next morning, we woke at four fifteen to catch a ferry across the river for a five o'clock bus to Dien Bien Phu, Vietnam. The bus waited on the other shore with cracked and hazy headlights, illuminating the path from water's edge to its door. The small boat (and I use this term *very* loosely), ferrying travelers from one shore to the other, almost left me behind. I was fairly unstable with my pack on, especially in situations that required balancing on one foot, especially when that one foot was in the bottom of an extra-long canoe. Nathan had hopped on easily. He was sitting comfortably at the front of the boat while the captain grabbed me by my head to steady my teetering. He used his grip to pull me into the boat. I was a little disappointed that Nathan hadn't even looked back to make sure I had boarded. I'm sure he would have enjoyed seeing a man grab my face with his fingers in my ears to support me. I couldn't stop giggling about it long enough to explain, in detail, what had happened.

The boat dropped us at the opposite shore, where we were assaulted by the smell of blood and the sharp smacks of a hatchet on cement. Apparently, the bus headlights were not only an aid to passengers, they were also providing enough light for the butcher to work. A water buffalo's carcass was splayed out on the cement, being chopped into choice cuts. I made a mental note to chew beef carefully the next time it was on the menu. Pieces of cement and small stones covered every ragged slice.

Chapter Three

Vietnam
Never. Stop. Moving.

Fellow backpackers liked to talk about the difficulties of travel in Vietnam. For the most part, what we had heard about Vietnam was negative. I was worried about it. We had heard how unfriendly people were, how pushy and impolite. We were expecting the worst.

We entered Vietnam in the mountains, at a border crossing only recently opened to foreigners, then continued on to Dien Bien Phu. We spent three days exploring old military museums, battle grounds, and monuments. It was where the last battle between the French and the Vietnamese took place in 1954, when Vietnam won her independence. It took me about two days to realize that the Vietnamese people are my favorite people. In the world. They have been fighting for their sovereignty for thousands of years. Since 111 BC, they have been invaded by China twenty-one times, by the French, by the United States, fought battles with Pol Pot's Cambodian Khmer Rouge and survived. They have thrived. The Vietnamese people are hard-working, ambitious, friendly, and some of the most open people I have ever met. I could not believe the negative things we had heard. I was surprised that anyone would complain of a bad experience in Vietnam.

Our plan was to head north to a town called Sapa. Ben and Deb had recommended it, calling it the Vietnamese version of Phongsaly. Considering our experience in Phongsaly, I'm surprised this appealed to us. It had rained the entire time we were there, but we figured it might be worth giving high altitude one more try.

Things moved a lot faster in Vietnam than they had in Laos. When a bus schedule said a bus would leave at five in the afternoon, it left at four fifty-eight. Vietnam was my kind of country. Nathan could no longer rely on his cotton watch to get us where we needed to be. In my opinion, if we weren't ten minutes early, we were late, and the Vietnamese agreed with me. The morning we left Dien Bien Phu, Nathan shocked me by saying, "Why don't we plan to get to the bus station a little early." He continued, "I'm willing to go early because I know how much you love waiting for transportation."

I didn't care what Nathan thought my reasons were for wanting to be early, so I confirmed his theory. "You are exactly right. I do *love* waiting for transportation. The more expensive it is, the more I love waiting for it."

From that point on, he was willing to arrive somewhere early, even if he himself did not deem it necessary, because he wanted me to be able to do the things that I loved.

Beer on the Go

Vietnam was by far the best value for our money. We used beer prices to determine the relative expense of all goods and services during our travel. A highly accurate and ingenious way to compare economies, if you ask me. In Vietnam, there existed the most glorious invention: the beer hall. This is something we did not see anywhere else, and had a hard time determining why, at first. For those of you who have never been to Vietnam, I'll explain. The beer hall is sometimes small, with two or three plastic children's lawn chairs and no table. Sometimes, it's very large, with dozens of kiddie tables and chairs, all about nine inches off of the ground. The Vietnamese are a little people, but not that little. I think they must enjoy being close to the earth because they use children's furniture whenever possible. Sometimes beer halls served Bia Hanoi in bottles, sometimes the beer came from kegs that were either filled by local brewers or transported from Hanoi in bulk. The concept of the beer hall is simple. It is a cheap, quick, and easy way to get a cold glass of beer. A typical pitcher of beer cost about a dollar, and a pint anywhere from seven to twenty-five cents. Men of all ages gather at the beer hall to eat peanuts, smoke cigarettes, and drink in the street. A beer hall isn't like a restaurant. The proprietor of each hall usually owns a tiny shop with barely enough room to store the beer, miniature furniture, and glasses. They open their doors and put their tiny furniture all over the sidewalk and sometimes into the street. Often, a vendor of dog meat or pho will set up shop next to these tables, to capitalize on the guaranteed business.

As a woman, I felt a little strange sitting at one of these establishments. I don't think we saw a single local woman drinking at a beer hall the entire time we were in Vietnam. I surmised that I was able to skirt this social taboo because I was an outsider.

So far, I'm sure the reader will agree that there seems no logical reason that beer halls wouldn't exist in the United States. Eventually, we witnessed the flaw.

We were enjoying an afternoon beer in the maze of streets behind our hotel, when a man pulled up to the beer hall on his moped. I don't know his exact words because he was speaking in Vietnamese, but by the reaction of the other men drinking beer, I would guess it was something like, *"Beer me!"*

The man didn't even bother to get off his bike. Traffic whizzed around him. The irritated grunts of other drivers could be heard over the engine revving as they moved to avoid his back tire, which jutted dangerously into their lane. The man pouring beer walked over to the moped with a full pint, and they exchanged money for libation. Without hesitation, the moped driver guzzled his entire drink, handed the glass back to the owner, and sped off into traffic.

Nathan and I shared a look, as invisible light bulbs started glowing above each of our heads. Maybe the beer hall was a phenomenon best kept locked in a place where traffic is better equipped to deal with idiots.

The traffic in Vietnam was an absolute pleasure to behold. At first, it looked like chaos. The more you watched and wove your way through it, the simpler it got. Never stop moving. If you stop, you die. The Vietnamese people have turned traveling on a street, with hundreds of cars and thousands of mopeds, in seven different directions, into a fluid and graceful art form. If everyone continues to move, no matter what, it becomes easy to determine the course they will take and how best to avoid hitting them. In a traffic pattern where sudden actions are forbidden, like stopping or swerving, it becomes immeasurably easier to navigate. As a pedestrian, the most fundamental lesson in crossing streets, whether one lane or ten, is not to panic. If the cars coming at you can tell that you are walking and that you do not plan to stop or change direction for anything or anyone, they can predict how *not* to hit you. If you panic or try to change your pace based on how fast cars are approaching, you face certain death.

I respected this system. Nathan was a little more prudent. He hated when I hopped out into a street with heavy traffic as though I was invincible. I felt it was necessary, if I wanted to blend in with the locals. Blending in was difficult because Vietnam was the land of straight and silky locks. My hair is wiry, curly, and big. It drew the attention of almost every Vietnamese woman in the country; they loved it. They stared at it, touched it, then let their children touch it. I was a good sport about the attention. It was like being a celebrity wherever we went. I don't think Nathan was jealous in the least. He was my dutiful bodyguard, making sure that women and children were the only ones bold enough to cop a feel. He did miss one teenage boy who sat behind me on a bus. The boy kept reaching his fingers through the seats and caressing my head. To say that this made me uncomfortable would be an understatement. It might not have been so bad had the boy possessed a single redeeming quality, but he was drooling and muttering and I couldn't see his other hand. To top it off, he had just cheated us out of almost ten dollars.

I was always looking for new ways to fit in. I bought myself a cloth face mask to protect my mouth and nose from slash and burn smoke, and the exhaust of city traffic. This accessory is a must-have for Vietnamese women. It protects their airways and their delicate skin from the blazing sun. I was certain that when wearing my face protection, it was impossible to discern my nationality. I likened my mask to Clark Kent's glasses. When I wore it, I was invisible. I chose to keep it tucked in my pocket during beer hall stops, to protect my Vietnamese identity. Only women from the outside can drink beer without social consequence.

Covert Ops

We split the trip to Sapa from Dien Bien Phu into two days. Our first six-hour bus ride left us in Lai Chau, where we spent the evening enjoying delicious local food, too much vodka, and the company of Ben and Deb. I made sure to clarify that we weren't stalking them when we showed up at the same hotel as they did, having bid them farewell the day before. I wasn't entirely certain they believed me. My eyes were wild, and I had a nervous twitch, both the result of my trip from the bus station to the hotel on the back of a moped taxi. I had clung to the moped driver for dear life as my full pack threatened to topple me from behind him. He sped erratically, swerving to miss potholes and giggling at his fortune: a lady-tourist wearing a skirt. If I had anticipated straddling a stranger on a moped, I probably would have taken a minute to put pants on, but it all happened so fast. Before I had time to assess the situation, Nathan was zipping away on the back of another moped. I thought it best to follow as quickly as possible. When I mentioned my displeasure at the experience, Nathan was surprised. "Really? I thought it was fun."

Because of his pack-weight to body-weight ratio, which was more conducive to maintaining balance on a swerving moped, his ride had been smoother than mine.

The next morning, we boarded a bus for Sapa. Ben and Deb were on the bus, as well as two other travelers from Holland. Each of us had been told a different price for the ride. The difference in price between the highest and lowest quote was less than one U.S. dollar. We all argued for about thirty minutes out of principle and for the mild entertainment it brought. When the bus driver's assistant, an aggressive woman on a power trip, finally got angry enough to grab Nathan's arm and threatened to throw him off the bus, (I didn't doubt she could have managed it), we paid the four-dollar fare. Ben and Deb also paid, but the Dutch couple played hard ball. They were dead set on paying three dollars and fifteen cents, not four dollars. They were cursed for their stinginess the entire journey. By the time we arrived in Sapa, the bus driver, having spent three hours listening to wealthy tourists refuse to cough up eighty-five cents, was in no mood to make any of our lives easier. He forced us off the bus a mile from town. As the man from Holland got off the bus triumphantly, his mortified girlfriend covertly paid the extra money for their tickets. Thanks to his antics, we had to walk for half an hour in the cold drizzle to find a hotel.

Sapa is known for being the home of the Hmong people. They live in villages outside of the city and bring their wares to sell in the market or on the streets. Most of the Hmong that we met were young women who'd walked considerable distances carrying woven bags and clothes to sell. They came to Sapa every day, to peddle their wares, in hopes of providing income for their families.

My first interaction with a Hmong woman went horribly. She approached Nathan and I as we were leaving our hotel to explore. Her brightly colored pink and green clothes were covered in embroidered designs of blue, orange, white, red, and yellow. There were several Hmong tribes in the area; each was easily identified by the color and style of its clothing. This woman was from the Flower Hmong village, about nine miles from Sapa. She carried a large satchel, packed with handcrafted bags, dresses, shirts, shawls, and trinkets. She had a friendly, gentle smile that came from her dark brown eyes as much as her lips and rosy cheeks. Her rounded face was framed by a vibrant shawl. I mistakenly entered into a binding contract to buy things I didn't want. I did this when I told the woman my name and smiled at her. This was as good as swearing on my mother's life that I would buy something. Even though I made it very clear that I was not interested, she became my shadow.

Hmong women spend hours following foreign women around, like desperate ex-boyfriends. They wait outside of restaurants, shops, and hotels while their mark goes about her day. They loiter around public bathrooms and ATMs. They are relentless. At every opportunity, they beg for attention, for the chance to show their crafts in hopes of a sale.

I was disturbed greatly by my stalker. After all, I had already informed her that I did not want to buy anything. At first, I assumed that I could pull a 007 move to ditch her. How hard could it be to leave a shop from a rear exit? I played at being a secret agent as a kid and had extensive experience spying on my brothers and parents without being caught. I considered myself skilled, if not an expert on covert maneuvers.

I was put to shame by the Hmong woman tracking me. She was a professional. After several hours of trying to get her to leave me alone, I stopped abruptly, and very firmly explained that she should follow someone else, because again, I was not interested. Her reaction led me to believe that she had misunderstood me. She stared at me with hatred and the fury of betrayal. Tears welled up in her eyes, and her mouth curled into a grimace. I looked down to make sure I hadn't stepped on her dog. I couldn't understand how she could be so angry. I had done nothing, that I knew of, to lead her to believe that I was interested. She began to berate me for being a crook and a liar. She explained that I had given her my promise, sworn to her with a smile, that her time would be well spent if she followed me. I had wasted her entire day. She was going to have to explain to her family that I had tricked her. A cold-hearted, Western woman had made a fool out of her. For someone who was not a native speaker, she had an excellent command of English expletives.

For many people, this tactic would have worked. They'd feel guilty and responsible. They'd look through the Hmong woman's things and pick out a few items to bring home as souvenirs. I had seen it happening on the street all day. Women, red faced with shame, sifting through a sack of items, handcrafted by the Hmong villagers. They were tourists defeated by guilt and manipulation. My stalker had underestimated me. I think manipulation, which is what the Hmong women were doing, exploiting the emotions of female Westerners, is deplorable. I refused to spend money reinforcing it. I felt sorry for the Hmong, they faced fierce competition to sell their goods and support their families. They walked great distances, in the rain and cold, and they never stopped working. But, our time in Sapa was significantly and negatively affected by the Hmong women's tactics. We were uncomfortable, and instead of being interested in their culture, we resented being treated like walking bags of cash. The whole experience left a bad taste in my mouth.

Our discomfort was not limited to the Hmong run-in; Sapa itself was dreary and cold. Low clouds and constant rain made it impossible to see the distant hillsides, terraced with rice fields. We stopped in at the tourist information building to look at pictures of the beautiful countryside. It seemed a pitiful way to experience Sapa, but it was the best we could do. We focused on enjoying local food and took advantage of the time to read and write, but it didn't take long for the damp chill to force us south.

We were sleeping on an overnight bus bound for Hanoi before we knew it.

Ice Cream Social

Chaos. Colorful, noisy, dangerous, chaos. In Hanoi, Nathan finally loosened up about traffic. On our first day in the city, we crossed dozens of busy streets and bustling intersections. He didn't even bother to look up when he stepped from the sidewalk. Out of necessity, I took on the role of prudent pedestrian, and saved his life more than once.

During one midday beer hall stop, we were thrilled to watch a local woman chop up a couple of smoked dogs. Perhaps more accurately, I was thrilled. If I hadn't just eaten, I would have been all over a dish of dog. It's hard to tell what breed you're dealing with when they're smoked, but I think it may have been a Welsh Corgi or a Jack Russell. To be sure, I took a picture and sent it to my college roommate, Kristin. She and her husband send out Christmas cards every year with pictures of their Corgi doing ridiculous things, like wearing a Santa cap, or driving a miniature sleigh. They seemed like the perfect people to ask for a definitive ID. It hadn't occurred to me that they might consider a picture of a smoked Corgi a threat. My dislike of this breed of dog was no secret.

On our third day in Hanoi, we witnessed something truly mysterious. At four in the afternoon we were on a walk in the French Quarter when all of a sudden, everyone was eating ice cream. Hundreds of people poured out of a warehouse we were walking past, all licking their waffle cone ice creams. Naturally, we walked in to investigate and get in on the action. Police were everywhere. Some had megaphones and were screaming into them. Motorcycles revved their engines from somewhere deep in the building. What appeared to be a gang was lounging in a dark, musty corner. At the opposite corner stood a group of five investment bankers wearing three-piece suits. The air was electrically charged, as though there was about to be a knife fight or something equally dangerous. Everyone was eating ice cream cones: gangsters, executives, little girls, and little old ladies. They all chatted with one another sociably while enjoying their icy refreshments. *Everyone* had one. We could not, for the life of us, find the source of the ice cream. People flooded out of the shadows, tattooed tough guys, scrawny academics, police officers. We were carried back into the daylight by a sated mob. We were the only people without ice cream and had no idea what was happening. Our best guess was that there was a mandatory, citywide ice cream social that the cops strictly enforced. It was at times like these that I wished we had spoken just a few words of Vietnamese.

The big city and its mysteries were a bit overwhelming, so we escaped for a few days to tour Halong Bay and Cat Ba Island, which sits about five miles off the coast. We thought about going to Cat Ba on our own, but then we heard rumors of a gang that made the lives of independent travelers miserable. Neither one of us was interested in confronting Vietnamese thugs, so we booked a three-day, two-night trip on an Indochina junk boat. Our first night would be spent on the boat in a private cabin and the second in a hotel on Cat Ba Island.

During our bus ride from Hanoi to the bay, our driver took some time to explain the legend of Halong. The name *Hạ Long* means *descending dragon* in Vietnamese. As the legend goes, there was once a great war fought between the Vietnamese people and seafaring invaders. The Vietnamese were fortunate to have the protection of the Gods, who saw fit to send a family of dragons to protect them. The dragons fought well and defeated the invaders with mighty blows from their spiked tails and razor-sharp claws. In the fight, much of the land was scraped and torn, leaving only jagged stone karsts and deep gouges. Over the centuries, the ocean water rose, leaving stone monoliths as the only evidence that a battle had been fought and won.

When we reached the docks, our driver hopped out of the van, pulled a four-foot, orange flag from behind his seat and held it above his head. We were told to follow the flag. It seemed like an unnecessary prop until he began speedily weaving through crowds of tourists toward our boat.

We boarded the junk boat with fourteen other people, just in time for a midday meal. As the boat lifted anchor and left its mooring, we enjoyed a mediocre rice dish with our new acquaintances. I don't remember where most of them were from, or their stories, but I do remember the three Norwegians on board. Two of them did not speak English at all. The third, a young man named Adelbert, spoke English fluently. He was more than happy to sit, chat, and sip beer with us above deck. I remember the Norwegians because of how perfectly they fit the stereotype of Norwegians. They seemed to operate through a thick haze. A glassy look and slow bodily movements made them almost cartoonish. Adelbert was fully aware of how the world perceived him and his fellow Norwegians. He joked, "The reason everyone thinks Norwegians are on drugs is that many of them are, at least the backpackers. But, not all of them are. My friends and I are just relaxed. We don't rush around or worry about schedules."

Nathan and I enjoyed Adelbert's description of traveling with two other Norwegians. He told us of missed bus connections, lost plane tickets, and expired visas. He seemed genuinely surprised to find himself and his companions on an organized trip. He shook his head, "We're generally not responsible enough to join tour groups. This is unusual."

Our conversation petered out as the boat sailed closer to the monstrous limestone karsts jutting from the water's surface. A hazy veil of mist enveloped us as we floated silently through thousands of stone fingers, reaching skyward from the depths of the ocean floor. As our boat slid through the water, new karsts appeared in the distance while those behind us faded.

I walked to the bow and sat with my feet dangling above white foam as it bubbled from deep slices opened by the forward momentum of our keel. Tiny droplets of moisture collected on my face and in my hair. My eyelashes were heavy with their weight. The ocean breeze and salty air were more refreshing than they had ever been. With the boat and its passengers at my back, I imagined myself flying alone through the legendary battlefield, watching dragons perch on the limestone structures towering above.

As the sun disappeared from the sky, we approached Cat Ba Island. There were five other junk boats dropping anchor in the same cove, all with passengers just like us, from all over the world. We settled down for an evening meal and some music with the crew. The cove was alive with the happy noise of strangers singing and dancing.

The next morning, our boat sailed toward the landing on Cat Ba. It sailed with excessive speed. Just before slamming into another boat and the cement pier, I heard Nathan scream from above deck, "*Hold on!*" I did, and thankfully so. Most passengers lost their footing as our vessel crushed the bow of the boat already unloading. The captain didn't seem bothered by the damage, nor did the police officer that watched the scene unfold. Captains are usually not the owners of these boats, so they are not especially distraught when the hull of one gets crushed by another. Exchanging insurance cards would just serve to get a fellow seaman in trouble. Therefore, they don't do it. We all hopped off the boat, receiving a friendly wave from our captain.

Our group of sixteen passengers hiked through the densely forested mountains in Cat Ba Island National Park, with a guide who was undeniably on drugs. He was tremendously entertaining. From what I could tell, he believed himself to be a miniature herbivorous creature. He didn't speak English, which made his authority as a guide utterly meaningless. He spent his time scurrying up vines and sitting twitchily on rocks while making strange noises. After the tour, a Frenchman sat next to us on the bus and whispered, "Did you see ze size of zat guy's pupils?!"

I nodded, "Yes. I suspect he was medicated. Heavily."

With our free time on Cat Ba Island, we rented a moped and packed our spelunking gear. More accurately, we packed a couple of headlamps and called them our *spelunking gear*. The first cave we found was behind someone's house. We paid seventy-five cents to have an eight-year-old girl unlock the gate protecting the cave. A small string of lights hung from the ceiling in the first three chambers. Past this illumination was nothing but blackness. We put on our headlamps and spent several hours exploring nooks and crannies that led deeper and deeper into the hillside. It's amazing how your adrenaline kicks in when you're inside a mountain and the only person who knows, has the attention span of an eight-year-old because she's an eight-year-old.

The second cave we found was Hospital Cave. A local man named Ba guarded it. Built during the Vietnamese–American war as a bunker and hospital, it featured a series of seventeen rooms buried inside a mountain. The facility was complete with a swimming pool, ping pong room, cinema, and several rooms for sleeping. Ba was stationed in the cave in 1979 during the Chinese occupation.

After our tour, we visited his house at the base of the cliff and taught him a few English words while we drank tea from shot glasses. We said goodbye to Ba with enough time to do a little more exploring before dusk.

We wanted to drive to the farthest reaches of the island before returning our rental moped. In part, we did it to explore, but we also wanted to use up as much fuel as possible. I know this isn't very environmentally conscious, but sometimes, for sanity's sake, a little gas guzzling can go a long way. Leaving gas in the tank of a rental bike was like bargaining for something in the market, then paying more than the agreed price because the vendor denies having change. We went to great lengths to avoid doing it.

Our junk boat travel companions all stayed in the same hotel as us. The next morning, the first mate joined us for breakfast. When he'd had his fill, he corralled us into another van and drove us back to the landing, where our captain waited.

The captain counted his passengers as we boarded. A look of concern came over him when he realized that three people who should have been aboard were not. Nathan and I looked around, even though we both already knew who was missing. Adelbert and his two companions were not on board. No one in the group had remembered seeing them since dinner the night before.

Two gentlemen from Germany muttered with breathy irritation, "Norwegians. Of course, it's the Norwegians."

We left without them.

Almos the Hungarian

Back in Hanoi, we continued our exploration on foot. One afternoon we stopped to get a bite to eat at a pho stall on our way to Ho Chi Min's Mausoleum. A man rolled up in a purple Honda Dream. He had stringy whitish hair that stood on end, giving him a recently electrocuted look. The hair that rested on his temples was tinted a subtle shade of pink, which made the flesh of his scalp less visible under thin patches. His name was Almos. He was a Hungarian man living and working in Hanoi. Judging by the leathery lines in his face, I guessed he was somewhere in his late sixties to early seventies. Nathan and I had just started slurping down our soups when Almos plopped down beside us.

Nathan used the expression, "Low hanging fruit" to describe something. This phrase began an inexplicable chain of events. Almos jumped out of his seat and almost his skin with excitement. He repeated the phrase with slow precision, "Low. Hanging. Fruit."

Then he grew much louder. *"Low hanging fruit!"* This is brilliant! I must remember this expression! *Low hanging fruit!"* His enthusiasm was bewildering.

In exchange for his newly acquired nugget of language gold, Almos did something interesting. He pulled out a stack of papers from his satchel. Each paper was exactly the same. There were hundreds of them. All were copies of a collage that looked to have been completed by a middle school student. He handed Nathan and I each a copy. Expectantly he asked, "Well, what do you think of *this*!? Please, give me your honest impressions."

I will never forget the image. It was two horses, face to face. One had reins being held by a teen girl, who was wearing leather chaps, a cowboy hat, and a belly shirt. Almos must have thought the belly shirt in poor taste because he scribbled over her mid-drift with black marker. We were both speechless. Silence lingered as we tried to figure out what was happening, while also appearing to thoughtfully appreciate the art.

I broke the silence, "Almos, what is this? Why do you have hundreds of copies in your bag?" Subtly isn't one of my strong suits. Thankfully, my query was not taken as insulting. Almos went on to tell a long-winded tale of a tortured artist named Cowboy. Cowboy apparently looked just like the woman in the picture but was a man. Almos was trying to gather objective comments about the image to report back to the artist. It was unclear whether the artist in question knew of Almos's project, or for that matter, Almos. It was also unclear whether Almos was mentally stable.

As if to prompt a speedier reaction, he said, "Also, you'd never guess it by looking at the picture, but the two horses are *actually* in *love*." Nathan left the commentary up to me. He just stared with wide eyes, trying to imagine what was going on in the strange man's head.

Almos gave us his cell phone number and made us promise to call him. He wanted us to either come to his house or meet him out for dinner before leaving Hanoi. We left the restaurant with smiles and handshakes.

Two days later, while Nathan and I were eating dinner, we started talking about recent events. We realized that neither one of us had spoken a word about the Almos-encounter to the other. Nathan was the first to offer an opinion, "I think something was wrong with that guy. Who carries around three hundred fliers to probe strangers about an artist's image? That doesn't even make sense. I got the impression that Cowboy was a figment of Almos's imagination."

We both had a good laugh. We had met enough nut jobs that Almos almost missed the cut as a topic of conversation. I had kept his phone number in my pocket on the off chance that we would muster the courage to risk being swindled in some way or captured in a Hungarian man's basement. Once we agreed that Almos may not have been sound of mind, I left the number in a hotel trash bin.

Despite being quite odd, our run-in with Almos and the participants of the mandatory ice cream social didn't scratch the surface of the strange things from which we tried to glean meaning. Hanoi was a city of many mysteries. Without any Vietnamese, discovering anything about our observations was a crude science. Much of our historical knowledge came from terrible English translations carved on monuments or engraved in temple walls. Our singular deciphering triumph came in Hanoi. We had visited a temple floating on an island in Hoan Kiem Lake. The theme of the temple was, shall I say, difficult to discern. Among other things, there was a giant statue of a red horse. It looked remarkably like Mr. Ed. I was momentarily distracted from our mission to gain insight by my need to take copious photographs of the horse's bulging eyeballs and gigantic teeth. When I was able to tear myself away from Mr. Ed, I found Nathan staring at an enormous turtle carcass. It was petrified somehow and surprisingly well preserved. Above the six-foot turtle, sat a stone obelisk. Carefully carved into its surface there was a story written in broken English. It never ceased to amaze me that stone monuments were carved by hand without first being checked by a native English speaker for spelling and grammar.

From what we were able to gather, a genius turtle lived in the lake. According to legend, this genius turtle teamed up with an 11th-century Vietnamese General to kick some Chinese ass with a sword that it strapped to its shell. At some point in history, this larger-than-life half-shell was betrayed, and the sword was stolen. In retaliation, it spent centuries wreaking havoc on its betrayers. As the Vietnamese tell it, the turtle was a real thorn in their side until they gave it back. The lake's name means, *restored sword lake*, in Vietnamese. The genius turtle most likely had an accomplice, a giant red horse. Perhaps it was a liaison for over-land campaigns. Naturally, after reading the account, I had some questions. How does a turtle strap a sword to its back? How does a turtle wreak havoc? Most important, how can anyone really know how smart a turtle is?

The dreadfully confusing pictographs accompanying the story did little to answer such questions.

At the time, what impressed me most was how hilarious the idea of a genius turtle was. We assumed that the translation had been wrong, but couldn't figure out what kind of turtle, if not a really smart one, was in the lake.

Several days after we learned of the genius cryptid, we found ourselves pushing through an excited mob on the shores of the Hoan Kiem. In the middle of the lake there were eight boats, manned by military personnel. There were twenty to thirty half-naked men screaming and jumping into the water, and a man wearing a three-piece suit, holding a megaphone. The boats were hovering around a net the size of a basketball court, and there were six men swimming inside of it at any given time. The man with the megaphone made us think it was a sporting event until the men in the water started frantically wrestling big bundles of net while screaming at one another. There was only one logical conclusion. They were catching the genius turtle! Unsurprisingly, they were having a difficult time. A smart turtle would know exactly what they were up to.

We watched this scene unfold for over two hours. Not once did we catch a glimpse of the turtle, or its sword. When the giant bundle of net, which may or may not have contained an aquatic creature, was wrestled into a boat, it was rowed to an island where a crane was set up. We wondered if the whole production might be a yearly morale building exercise for the Vietnamese government.

"The turtle still lives!"

Maybe it was a Groundhog's Day-esque exercise where the weather or harvests depended on the turtle's ability to see its shadow, but even when the bundle reached the crane, we were left without a visual. The roads were blocked off, police were keeping kids from acting up, and there were tens of thousands of people. It was a big deal. I suppose we could have asked someone what was happening, but that would have taken all the fun out of sleuthing.

We were a bit stunned when we learned the real story several days later. Our guess had been, for the most part, correct. We had witnessed a six-foot-long, genius tortoise being hauled from a polluted lake for medical treatment. It was suffering from lesions and general poor health. No one knew for sure whether the tortoise was a *Rafetus swinhoei*, in which case it was one of four remaining on the planet, or another closely related species with no other surviving members. It must have hidden the sword for safe keeping because we didn't hear anything about that.

Ticket ≠ Seat

One week was enough time spent in Hanoi. We packed our bags and walked to the train station to catch a ride to Ninh Binh, a small town with little to offer except its central location to several nearby attractions. The Hanoi train station brought us face to face with one of the greatest challenges a Westerner must overcome in Vietnam: ticket counters.

Nathan and I each chose a separate ticket line in the hopes that one of us would be better than the other at getting to the front. The people of Vietnam do not see the virtue in forming lines. Not even a little. I felt my skin getting tingly when a swarm of young women shamelessly snuck their way in front of me. Nathan was having similar issues in his line. Somehow, after starting third, he was sixth. We were helpless. As Americans, we are programmed from the age of five that line cutting is not an acceptable behavior. Children are required to pay serious fines for even the smallest line infraction. All members of a line that has been violated will speak up to defend the integrity of that line. The sneak who tried to break the code is sent to the back with shame, or worse, banned from the establishment. In Vietnam, this Western mentality is laughable. Waiting in line is for weaklings.

Self-doubt will get you nowhere in the face of a Vietnamese ticket counter. I had a breakthrough when I let my irritation bubble to the surface. My hand shot to the counter in front of me, blocking the women to my left. The low growl that rumbled from my throat made the woman behind me laugh uncomfortably, then back away. As an outsider, you have to sow the seeds of doubt in the crowd around you. The doubt that makes them ask themselves, "Is this foreigner about to do something crazy?" Ideally, they will conclude that the answer is, "Yes."

I triumphantly bought our tickets on the first train to Ninh Binh. Once there, we rented a moped to explore the national parks and temples in the area. Our excitement at having overcome the ticketing counter obstacle was short lived. We fell victim to a moped rental trick, perpetrated by our hotel receptionist. We rented a bike for the day, filled it up with gas, used it, and left about two-thirds of a tank for the next day. We made it clear we would be renting again in the morning.

The next morning came, and as promised we rented the same bike. Its gas tank was empty. The manager had siphoned out the remaining gas and sold it back to the station. Usually, Nathan lets tricks like this roll off his back, but this swindle, for some reason, struck him as particularly heinous. He walked back into the hotel and demanded, "Are you serious? Where the *hell* is the gas we put in the tank *yesterday*?"

To the hotel manager's credit, he had multiple tricks up his sleeve. He had the audacity to pull a classic move used by all tourists at one time or another. He acted as though he had no idea what we were talking about. This made it impossible to get anywhere. It was like ranting to a wall. He had clearly been paying close attention to the strategies travelers used to avoid tough situations.

"Oh, you need gas?" He said, "The station is down the street and to the left."

"No. I don't need gas. I bought gas yesterday. Where is it?" Nathan demanded.

"Where is it? The station is down the street and to the left."

Brilliant.

When we first arrived in Dien Bien Phu, I had been shocked by the negative things we had heard about Vietnam. I hadn't been able to comprehend why other backpackers felt so jaded by their experiences, but I was beginning to understand the sentiment.

Most people from developed countries are not prepared to deal with Vietnamese business practices. It is easy to take tricks like siphoning a gas tank, or raising prices for certain customers, personally. In Vietnam, it's not personal. It's business. Tourists often feel that they're being cheated because they don't understand this. Their constant fear of being taken advantage of diverts their attention away from enjoying the experience and turns them into paranoid crabs. These people are the ones arguing about a one-dollar price hike on a five-hour bus ride, or a scrambled egg that cost them thirty-five cents instead of thirty. They are the kind of tourists that I support swindling. They deserve it. Nathan and I tried to balance our frustration at being susceptible to scams with an acceptance that sometimes paying more was worth helping someone in need. We tried not to hold anything against people trying to squeeze money from our pockets. They were doing their best to feed their families. It was a balance that could be exhausting.

I found that even the most despicable extortion couldn't bring me to tears. Only once did I come close. We got ourselves a heck of a deal on sleeper-bus tickets, half price, leaving Ninh Binh and heading to the demilitarized zone (DMZ). Fourteen dollars for a twelve-hour ride, with beds and a bathroom on board. A great deal!

I guess we made a rookie mistake when we assumed that we were buying actual beds on this sleeper-bus. The bus was moving before we realized that every bed was taken and there were already three people sleeping on the floor. No person in their right mind would choose to sleep without a blanket or pillow on a bus floor that smelled like a swamp, for twelve hours, but we didn't have a choice. I tried to stay upbeat, laughing at the absolute absurdity of our situation. Nathan made the best of it and hunkered down to sleep. It was about an hour into the journey that my despair took hold. I began to feel the contents of my stomach make their way up my esophagus. I don't normally suffer from car sickness. Then again, I don't usually pick low lying, cramped bus floors to cuddle with the wet, suffocating stench of feet — so I've never really, I mean *really* tested my susceptibility to motion sickness. It did not help my situation that the bathroom on board was within four feet of my spinning head and twisted gut. I could have sworn that every passenger on that bus emptied the contents of their colon at least twice on the trip.

 The bus stopped in Dong Ha, a town that was moved during the Vietnam War to make room for an American military base. We got off the bus and hired a tour guide that spoke English to take us to the DMZ. He was eighteen when the Vietnam War was coming to a close and had enlisted with the South. The driver, our guide's boss, was a soldier who fought for the North. It proved to be a very interesting dynamic. Our guide, Hoa, explained that the Americans moved he and his family to a village that had been constructed for the people displaced by the military base. He said the conditions were good, and that his family felt safe and protected. He showed us a picture in the military museum just across the river, in what was Viet Cong territory. It had a caption reading, "Southern villagers were moved to concentration camps by American soldiers."

 He rolled his eyes and whispered, "Propaganda."

 Hoa then took us to Vin Moc, the infamous tunnel network and underground village, just north of the DMZ. We explored the expansive network of tunnels, winding in all directions beneath the ground. I could stand upright in almost every tunnel, but Nathan had a much harder time getting around. We both marveled at the incredible fortress.

The determination and heart of the Vietnamese people astounded me. A sign that hung near one of the tunnel entrances said simply, "We choose to live." The villagers of Vin Moc had seen no other way to survive than to go underground. They'd spent two years digging two miles of tunnels between thirty and ninety feet beneath the earth's surface. Sixty families lived within the tunnels, which contained kitchens, wells, hospital rooms, and living quarters. Seventeen babies were born in the darkness.

The Chubby Girl Wants to Walk

From the DMZ, our guide took us south to the nearest tourist attraction, the city of Hue. We found a hotel where we could be comfortable, and I spent the next week in bed with strep throat. The sleeper-bus ride from hell had been my undoing. I couldn't say for sure, but I suspected that breathing in the dank stench of sweaty feet for twelve hours had given me a terrible respiratory and throat infection. Nathan accused me of giving it to him when he came down with the same fever and raw throat. I maintained that I had done no such thing. If anything, he had *taken* it from me with his habit of toothbrush swapping. He began to collect disposable toothbrushes from every hotel we visited. Unfortunately for the environment, he never used the same toothbrush for more than two nights until we stepped back onto American soil.

In Hue, we spent our sick days napping and reading. Several weeks earlier when we were in Hanoi, I had picked up a book about cultural do's and don'ts, which I finally had time to read. Among other things, it said that the Vietnamese people consider licking one's fingers after a good meal or after eating a piece of fruit, or for any other reason, bad form. It's called eating like a cat. I laughed when I read this because I ate like a cat all the time. I was particularly feline when there was melted chocolate involved. I believe I learned the hard way that eating like a cat makes you sick as a dog, at least in Vietnam. Luckily, antibiotics were an over-the-counter, non-prescription-requiring purchase. I spent almost a month eating amoxicillin like candy.

The sleeper-bus incident gave me an appreciation for scammers, something I never thought I would have. When scammers scam scammers, I find myself in the awkward position of rooting for the scammer trying to scam my scammer. I feel an example might be necessary. Two sweet, hardworking maids covertly approached Nathan and I at our door one evening. They asked if we would let them do our laundry under the table for the same price as the hotel charged (twice the local rate), without alerting the reception desk. I enthusiastically shook their hands, nodded my approval and handed over our things. It gave me great pleasure to be complicit in a scam of scammers.

Being sick in a foreign country is much worse than being sick at home. When you're home, you know just the thing that's going to make you feel better. Ginger ale is available at the grocery store or local gas station, and a comfortable couch with a big screen TV and DVD player are only as far away as your living room. In Hue, I was trapped in a tiny hotel room with a poorly functioning air-conditioning unit, blankets that smelled like rancid cheese, and a window that didn't open. I was nauseated at the idea of eating rice and fish sauce to regain my strength. In a fit of anger and frustration, I told Nathan that I would literally strangle someone for a saltine cracker. Strangle to *death*. He felt slightly better than I did, so he left quickly to find whatever comfort food was available. He locked the door behind him.

Being bedridden for almost a week gave me some time to reflect. As I think is common with invalids, I daydreamed about better times. I craved home. I imagined myself being comfortable and having friends and family to take care of me. It was the first time I felt a twinge of home sickness. I remembered all the things

I was so lucky to have at home, and I missed every one of them dearly.

I was lucky to have Nathan too. I felt a little guilty for making him believe I was homicidal for saltines. I couldn't imagine how difficult sickness was for those people traveling alone.

When we finally felt up to exploring Hue, we took a long walk in the park. The streets were teeming with tourists. In the hot afternoon sun, many of them hired a moped or a rickshaw to cart them around. This meant that drivers were waiting at every corner, all excited to win our business. They each tried mightily to persuade us *not* to walk. One of these moped drivers, who was offering a trip to any destination for real cheap, yelled out to me.

"Get on my bike! Where you go? I take you there."

I responded like I always did. I told him that I liked walking and that I enjoyed the exercise. At this point, his salesmanship failed him.

"You look heavy. It's too hard to walk. You should sit. Walking for you looks difficult."

Even though I was certain he understood a mere fraction of my reply, I couldn't help but address his unwitting dig.

"Listen pal, you try eating noodles and bread three times a day as a Caucasian woman. I may have put on a few pounds, but I assure you my legs can still support my weight."

When Nathan was able to stop his laughing, he pulled me in for a hug and a kiss on the cheek. After that incident, I was ready to move on.

From Hue, we traveled south in small steps. First, we stopped in Da Nang, then Hoi An. Each city had a unique charm to it; with each stop, we became less and less intimidated by the prospect of not knowing anything when we arrived.

Over 500 tailors call Hoi An home, so we chose one woman with a good sense of humor and excellent English to design jackets for each of us. While we waited for our new clothes, we visited the Angkor Wat of Vietnam, a series of ancient Cham ruins in My Son. Just south of Hoi An, we stopped in Quy

Nhon, where we enjoyed long walks on the beach and the peace that comes with visiting a town not yet on the tourist map. When we had sufficiently recovered from the hubbub of one heavily trafficked city, we were ready to dive into another.

Cyclo Killer, Qu'est-ce Que C'est?

We decided on an afternoon train from Quy Nhon to Nha Trang. The train was scheduled to leave just before 5 p.m., so we grabbed our bags around three, to leave plenty of time to either walk to the train station or get a lift on a moped taxi. The first two moped taxi drivers refused to give us a fair price, so we started to walk. We had a two-mile trek ahead of us, it was blisteringly hot, and we each carried at least fifty pounds on our back. We were extremely motivated to find another couple of drivers to haggle with.

An eighty-nine-pound man, who had an expression I first confused with inebriation and later understood as desperation, approached us. He had been eavesdropping on our bargaining session with the two guys on mopeds and agreed to take us where we wanted to go, for the price we had offered the others. He was dressed in a sweat-stained button-down shirt, with a ball cap awkwardly balanced on a mat of straggly hair that hung in knots down to his shoulders. He had a reassuring smile that immediately put us both at ease.

Then we saw how small his cyclo was. The cyclo, also called a rickshaw, is an adapted bicycle with what could be likened to a medieval wheelchair strapped to the front of it. We gave him four raised eyebrows indicating we needed some clarification on what it was he was offering. Both of us? Both bags? At the same time? Where? He helped us arrange ourselves and our packs on his cyclo, then hopped on the back. Nathan was sitting on top of his bag which was balanced precariously on top of me. I was hunched over with my chest resting on my knees, and my bag was crammed beneath my feet, which were somehow above my head. We were an absolute spectacle.

Things went downhill. Unfortunately, not literally. The man started to peddle. Our first thirty feet of movement, across six lanes of traffic, happened over the course of approximately two minutes. Nathan's groans persisted the entire time. He insisted that we get off and walk because walking would surely be faster. To me, it seemed like changing our minds might come across as an insult to the tiny man's ability to do his job. Finally, we picked up some speed as the cyclo-hero swung his entire body side to side, using all of his weight to rotate the pedals.

We were laughed at and heckled the entire ride. We felt awful listening to the labored breathing of a man killing himself to haul our 100 pounds of crap and 250 pounds of lazy flesh across town. It was, by far, the most guilt-filled, embarrassing experience I can remember having. When the cyclo finally pulled over to let us out, we paid the poor man his dollar fifty. He took it with a shaky hand. As he stood on wobbly legs, gasping for breath and dripping sweat, we didn't have the heart to ask him where on earth we were, because it wasn't the train station. Instead, we smiled and thanked him profusely. When he had peddled out of sight, we pulled out a map. He had taken us only slightly closer to our destination. Hiring another ride felt wrong, so we decided to walk the remaining mile. It seemed like the least we could do as penance for having almost killed a man.

When we arrived in Nha Trang later that evening, we were suckered by the fourth-floor trick. This is a shrewd move by receptionists to con hotel guests. They tell you that the only room they have is on the fourth floor. You have to trudge up a miserably narrow staircase (because the elevator is broken) with your life strapped to your back, to look at the accommodations. By the time you reach the top, you are so tired that you'd accept a rug on the floor as long as it meant getting to put your bag down. We took the room.

Nha Trang was a city on the beach, so we didn't spend much time exploring it. Instead, we swam, sunbathed, and ate as much Western food as we could get our hands on.

In my life, I had never heard anyone mention vacationing on the beaches of Vietnam. I suppose that's partly because I've never been interested in vacationing for tanning opportunities, but it might also be that most Americans don't know about Vietnam. The beaches in Nha Trang made me reconsider my opposition to paying loads of money for a plane ticket to a white sand beach where tourists lie around in the sun for a week, doing nothing but eating, drinking, reading, and crisping.

The sand stretched for miles in both directions. Where it met the water's edge, it changed from fluid, white grains to an almost transparent crystalline glass. The saturated surface was cool on the bottoms of our feet and melted around our toes. Palm trees lined the lush grass that grew between the beach and the busy street, buffering the angry sounds of traffic and business. On the beach, we were able to relax completely, and let the sun dry our salty bodies.

The Nha Trang waterfront was serene in a way that no beach in southern Thailand was. In Thailand, there were hundreds, maybe thousands of tourists littering every stretch of sand. In Vietnam, there were so few people that we could spend two hours swimming in the surf without catching a glimpse of another tourist. It didn't seem possible that such a beautiful place could be so deserted.

After a couple of days of gluttony and sloth, we decided to head inland for another bike trip. This time we rented a single, slightly sturdier motorcycle for the two of us. We left Nha Trang heading west, into the Central Highlands, on the Ho Chi Min highway.

Easy Riders

The first leg of our motorcycle journey put us in Paradise, a bungalow guesthouse located on DocLet Beach. The resort was located at the tip of a peninsula with something against street signs, and in some places, streets. We had driven around salt flats for much of the afternoon, praying we wouldn't be reduced to sleeping in a salty ditch. Our skin was a deep shade of pink and our eyes were bloodshot from wind and sun exposure. Just as we were losing hope, we stumbled into Paradise, its lavish gardens, free drinks, and ocean breezes made it worthy of the name. Our bungalow came with three meals a day and turquoise, bath-water waves. We spent the next day recovering on our porch, admiring the postcard quality seascape while sipping mango shakes.

Two days later we rode to Buon Ma Thuot, the coffee capital of Vietnam. We had only recently discovered that the Vietnamese coffee we loved so much was roasted in butter. Buon Ma Thuot was a city sprinkled with coffee shops at every corner. It was the perfect venue for our coffee tasting tour. We drank cup after cup of buttery joe. It didn't occur to me at the time, but this is probably the reason that Nathan started to get seriously finicky about his sun exposure. Our dwindling sunblock supply and his consumption of obscene amounts of caffeine made him crazy. He was cheerful and relaxed when the sun went down, or when he was covered head to toe in clothing, but when even the smallest part of his already burned body was exposed to the sun, he went into a caffeine-induced frenzy. He became irritable and jittery on the motorcycle, which as his passenger, I found terrifying.

We took one day to explore Buon Ma Thuot and its surroundings. It didn't go as smoothly as we would have liked. We spent much of the morning looking for sunblock to calm Nathan's nerves, but were unsuccessful. The only lotion available in cities that didn't see many tourists was skin-whitening lotion. The Vietnamese don't use sunblock. They wear clothes, and if they accidentally get a tan, they bleach it away with whitening lotion. When I tired of jumping from the back of the motorcycle to search for UV protection, which usually required a mimed demonstration of being burned alive by the sun, I gave up. We suffered the rest of the sweltering day in our long sleeve shirts and long pants. We had heard about a waterfall and a national park with an incredible, 1,500-foot suspension bridge that hung above the jungle. Our intention was to explore both before leaving the area, but we couldn't find them. We drove back and forth along a fifteen mile stretch of road three times, trying to locate a single indication that the park or waterfall existed. Nathan was reaching the end of his endurance in the afternoon heat, and I was frustrated that we had wasted an entire day driving around looking for things and not finding them.

Nathan made an executive decision as chief navigator, to go with his gut. If I had been alone, I would have given up and gone back to town for an ice cream, but Nathan was in no mood to give up. He pointed to several mountains in the distance. "You see those two mountains? I think the waterfall is somewhere around them. To have a waterfall, you have to have a mountain. We're going to find it."

I gave his middle a supportive squeeze. What was the worst that could happen? He ignored everything we were told about the location of the waterfall and drove us deep into the jungle. I was nervous as we bumped our way over pothole-riddled logging paths, running through the middle of nowhere. A flat tire would have meant a night in the jungle, most certainly. Nathan's disturbing sense of direction coupled with luck, delivered us to the falls. We arrived at a back gate. The ticket saleswoman seemed surprised to see us. She eyed our dusty faces and sweat-soaked clothes with confusion, then pointed questioningly in the direction from which we had come. We both nodded and smiled. She shook her head with disbelief and passed us our tickets. We were the only people in the park, which was becoming the norm for us. The waterfall was beautiful, though not as large as it would have been in the wet season. We licked most of a chocolate bar from its wrapper and dipped our heads into the cool water to revive ourselves. After a quick hike to the top of the waterfall, we found ourselves wandering through an expansive coffee plantation.

It was the kind of discovery that made the hassle of exploring without a guide worth it. We meandered through acres of red berried coffee bushes, plucking ripe beans and testing them between our teeth, which incidentally, I would not recommend to anyone. Coffee is roasted for good reason. We were seeing things that most people would never be lucky enough to see.

We took another road on the return trip to Buon Ma Thuot. It was much shorter and for the most part, paved.

Besides a sore posterior, I felt refreshed the next morning when we climbed back onto our motorcycle to hit the road. Our next stop was DeLat, a city that had served as a refuge to the French during the early eighteenth century.

About halfway to DeLat, we realized we were never going to make the trip in a single day. We hadn't known the exact mileage of the drive, but it became evident that DeLat was out of reach when the sun started to set. We saw our first mile marker in the dusk; our destination was still over seventy miles away. This may not seem far, but we had been on the bike for almost eight hours, dodging school children, farm animals, and other drivers, and were in no condition to push on in the dark.

In desperation, we took a side road that looked promising because it wound its way around a lake. In the distance, we could see structures lining the bank. It seemed like the perfect place to build a hotel complex.

When we found it, we were both pleasantly surprised that it was what we had desperately hoped it would be, a luxurious hotel campus with cottages lining the picturesque lake, each equipped with a porch, a magnificent bathtub and cable television. It was almost too good to be true.

We booked a room and were led down a cobblestone path through opulent gardens and past an exotic outdoor hot tub, carved from stone. The verdant grounds were expertly manicured. We arrived at the door of a small cottage overlooking the lake. While we stood admiring our quaint accommodation, the mousy woman who had shown us the way, disappeared before we could thank her.

I pleaded for the first shower. Nathan nodded his head weakly, then collapsed onto the bed. The bathroom was a work of art. The walls were covered in a colorful, mosaic flower pattern, crafted from thousands of pieces of tile and glass. The shower and bathtub were sparkling white porcelain, and the floors were slate with royal blue mortar. I was in heaven.

Midway through my shower I heard a loud crash in the bedroom. Nathan yelled, "We have a bit of a situation in here!" Then another loud noise and frantic rustling. I jumped out of the shower and dried off as fast as I could. When I emerged from the steamy bathroom, wrapped in my oversized towel, the room was chaos. Nathan was shoving toilet paper under the front and back doors, locking windows and throwing shoes at the walls.

Thousands of flying termites and wasps were creeping into the room through every possible crack. They came in endless streams through the windows, under doors, through the AC unit mounted near the television, and somehow, from the ceiling above our beds. Nathan was trying to stop them with toilet paper, towels, and our shoes. I joined in the fight by removing my towel and shoving it under the back door. The buzzing was all around us. The snap snap of little termite necks could be heard over and over, as they flew toward the light, and hit glass. In the short time that it had taken me to shower, the sun had gone down. We were under attack. The only way to stop the assault was to turn off the lights, but we hadn't set up our mosquito nets yet. We needed the light to do it. When we had finally done all that we could to stem the flow, we focused our energy on killing the intruders. They covered the floor like a thick rug, climbed into our open backpacks, and buzzed in our pillowcases. One or two termites are harmless. One or two thousand termites are horrifying. It took us the better part of two hours to clear one of the two twin beds, the floor, and our packs.

We assembled the mosquito net over the cleared bed and looked around one last time, to make sure our defenses would hold.

Then we saw it.

Above the door, a mere two inches from where Nathan's head had been moments before, hung the largest spider I had ever seen. I screamed. I had falsely assumed that spiders as large as the one in our cottage were cinematic creations, mere science fiction. When Nathan saw the source of my terror, he too screamed like a little girl. We were both frozen. I was still naked. Having fought comfortably for two hours in the buff, it struck me a little strange that I suddenly felt incredibly vulnerable. The spider was the size of a rat. Its hairy black body didn't move like I expected it to. It didn't casually wander the walls, stepping gently with its eight furry appendages. It jumped. It jumped with lightning speed and with ferocity. It wanted blood. We were exhausted from our termite battle, but both realized that we wouldn't sleep a wink if the spider were left alive. Nathan turned to me, keeping one eye on the spider, "We won a battle, but not the war."

I might have laughed, had the circumstances not been so dire. We each grabbed the heaviest object we could find, a hiking boot and a book. On the count of three, we threw our items with deadly intent. The crash shook our entire cottage. When the dust settled, we slowly approached our fallen weapons. Nathan poked at his hiking boot with a water bottle while simultaneously jumping backwards in anticipation of a retaliatory attack. Nothing. The spider had not landed with the shoe or the book. It was nowhere to be found. It had disappeared into thin air.

We did the only thing we *could* do. We hastily doubled the mosquito net, crawled into a single twin bed, and huddled in the dark, listening for any sign of the intruder. We both laid awake for hours trying to calm our itchy skin and overactive imaginations.

The next morning, we packed carefully, making sure to shake our clothes and empty our shoes. The carnage was hard to believe. Outside, the windowsills were stacked two inches deep with termites huddling for a glimpse of the light within. The back porch wasn't visible through the broken brown bodies, and our room was littered with dead insects. We were fatigued, grumpy, and happy to say goodbye to our Jekyll and Hyde cottage. I was considerably less friendly to the receptionist while checking out. The hotel staff had to have known what we would experience, yet they gave no sign of sympathy or guilt.

The road turned to absolute garbage soon after we were on our way. The potholes were so big and so frequent that Nathan had to drive much more slowly than the day before. I think he enjoyed practicing his evasive maneuvers for the first hour. The swerving and brake slamming were somewhat reminiscent of video game derby races, but after nearly flipping into a gully of jagged rocks, the ride became a chore instead of a game. Long sections of sharp crushed rock caused the bike to slide wildly. If I had been the one driving, we would have crashed a dozen times over. I was worried that we had taken a wrong turn, considering there had not been a single sign along the way. Nathan didn't share my rising panic or empathize with the worry tightening my chest. He didn't seem concerned at all. I couldn't fathom how he managed to navigate through the jungle on hunches.

We bumped into some Easy Riders after surviving a particularly harrowing stretch of road. These gentlemen are a popular form of transport for tourists with an adventurous streak and some extra cash. The Easy Riders are motorcyclists that charged between fifty and seventy-five dollars a day to drive their passengers through rural Vietnam. For people unwilling or unable to drive their own bike, it isn't a bad option.

Our bike rental costs us seven dollars a day. Surprisingly few tourists try this trip on their own, probably because of the conspiracy to hide all useful maps and directional indicators from outsiders. We took wrong turns almost sixty percent of the time. Thankfully, it was easy to discover our errors when they delivered us to someone's back yard, or a field inhabited by water buffalo. When we met the Easy Riders with their charges holding on behind them, they offered to show us a shortcut the rest of the way to DeLat. We happily followed. We hadn't been aware of a short cut. Truthfully, we hadn't been aware of the long way either.   DeLat was even more beautiful than we had expected. Built as a resort town, its charming villas and boulevards tucked themselves into the mountains of the Central Highlands. There were gardens everywhere, flowers lining the streets, and blue skies. The color of the sky was shocking. We hadn't realized how much the smog and smoke from slash and burn farming had been distorting the colors of life in the lowlands. DeLat was clean. The air was crisp, and the colors of everything around us glowed vibrantly.

The Easy Riders showed us to an inexpensive hotel and wished us luck. As an afterthought, they asked if we wanted to join them and their passengers for an evening of karaoke. We agreed. It was the perfect opportunity to learn what the Vietnamese people found so enjoyable about screaming into a microphone.

That evening we were thrilled to have accepted the invite. The Vietnamese karaoke experience is unparalleled. We had been hearing muted voices through walls and from behind closed doors since our arrival in Dien Bien Phu. The voices were usually pained with lost love or proudly patriotic, and almost always, they were singing off key. For a language with five tones, it surprised me how few native speakers could apply them to music. For some reason, we had never ventured out to find their source.

With our posse of Easy Riders, we walked up to one of the many buildings with the word karaoke painted on the side of it. We all filed up a narrow staircase to the sixth floor. At the top of the staircase, there was a single door leading to a tiny room. The room had no windows and no ventilation, which in hindsight, was a serious design flaw. Inside the room, a wraparound couch made of fake leather hugged the walls. The television was rigged with surround sound; its speakers hung in every corner. A woman appeared in the doorway carrying two cases of beer, snacks, and two microphones. We crowded into the room with our new friends, who had all apparently skipped dinner to hit the bottle. Cigarette smoke filled the air as the song books were passed around.

Nathan and I had realized weeks before that in Vietnam, fitting in was all about losing inhibitions. We didn't have alcohol to loosen our tongues like our friends did, but that didn't stop us. I can't speak for Nathan, but a strange exhilaration, a kind of letting go occurred when I found myself in such a new and overwhelming situation. As the night wore on, the Easy Riders became more animated, dancing wildly, cursing, smoking, and spilling bottles of beer all over themselves. They were celebrating like there would never be another night of karaoke. It no longer mattered that I was embarrassed to sing in front of Nathan. It didn't matter that I couldn't speak Vietnamese, or that I had only just met the room full of motorcyclists. Like everyone else, I sang. I sang loudly, off key, and vigorously. Nathan stood and belted out ballads with his arm around a Vietnamese man whose words slid sloppily past the cigarette pinched between his lips. I performed a soulful duet with another Easy Rider, swaying lovingly as we crooned, "Everything I do, I do it for you."

That night, I believe we began to understand our destiny. We were on the path to becoming exceptional tourists.

Bangkok-ed Again?

Our second night in DeLat, we paid three times the listed price for our hotel room. Why? It was the anniversary of the end of the Vietnam War, and the start of a thirty-six-year stretch of peace. Our hotel receptionist informed us that things were going to get crazy. There was going to be a Peace Festival. It sounded like something worth sticking around for, so we did.

People from all over Vietnam did show up, but other than extra street-food vendors, higher prices, a few musical performances, and chaotic traffic, it didn't feel much like a festival. We concluded that, during *huge* festivals, the Vietnamese people celebrate by milling around. We took extreme measures to investigate this phenomenon. We started tailing people. What better way to figure out what draws locals to the streets than to pick up a mark at the parking garage and follow him around? This proved unsuccessful for three reasons.

1. *I am the worst detective in history. I kept getting too close, making eye contact, and bumping into my mark.*
2. *I got bored. My attention to our detective work waned after about ten minutes of tailing a man who did nothing but mill around.*
3. *Covert operations are difficult in Asia for someone who is white, and has a giant, curly afro. If locals weren't suspicious the first time the saw me, they most certainly were the second time.*

We gave up on following people around when I caught sight of a vendor selling both donuts and coconut milk. By the time we finished our snack, the streets were beginning to empty. Ten thirty, and the festival was winding down. On our walk back to the hotel, a thought struck us. Was it possible that the Peace Festival story was a ruse? A ruse to triple hotel prices, jack up the cost of transportation, and persuade us to stay? It felt a lot like the scam we had discovered in Bangkok. The one that took advantage of tourist ignorance by convincing foreigners that every day was Buddha Day, a holiday worth sticking around for. Was it possible that the so-called Peace Festival was really a typical Saturday night? We would never know.

One night of exorbitant hotel prices was enough. We traveled back to Nha Trang where we had left our large packs to collect them and continue south. After returning our rental motorcycle, we felt it was worth spending another day in town to organize our own transportation south. Upon our return, our hotel receptionist informed us that she had already booked tickets for us on a train to Ho Chi Min City for twenty dollars apiece. We had not asked for this or wanted it. We told her to un-book the ticket, then made a point of letting her know that we were going to rent bicycles and ride them to the train station to check prices. She appreciated our ambition about as much as we appreciated her chicanery.

First, we peddled to the train station to gather information. It took some work, but we discovered a list of set prices well hidden from outsider eyes. The true cost of the twenty-dollar train ticket was seven dollars. Next, we went to the bus station where we uncovered the list of bus fares for locals, from Nha Trang to Ho Chi Min. The public buses were booked, but we found a private bus company close to our hotel. We called them from the bus station. Instead of *asking* the price of the sleeper-bus, we *stated* the price. The man selling tickets groaned and asked if we had been to the bus station. Victory!

It was well worth braving the afternoon heat to hear the defeat in bus-ticket-man's voice as he agreed to the price of our ticket. I had learned to be cautious with victory, so before handing over our money, I made sure to clarify that if there were no beds for us on the sleeper-bus that I would be getting my money back. The ticket man laughed, then when I didn't, he nodded his head seriously, "There are beds."

The ride was as smooth as we could have expected. I dared to hope we had escaped our lousy luck with buses, as I stretched my well-rested body and waited for our bags to be pulled from the underside of the sleeper-bus. When our packs hit the pavement with loud *splats* it was evident we had not. Apparently, the plumbing from our onboard toilet needed some work. Our bags, Nathan's more so than mine, were soaked with urine.

Hello Ho Chi Min!

We found a hotel as fast as we could. An elderly woman corralled us into her guesthouse and pointed us up a dark staircase. We had a look, found the room satisfactory, and agreed to stay. She didn't seem to notice that we smelled like toilet bowls, which probably should have tipped us off to her poor observational skills. We didn't bother changing our clothes, since we were already wearing the least urine-soaked items we owned. Instead, we locked our new room and headed out in search of some fresh coffee and a hot breakfast. As we left, we handed over everything inside of our packs, and the packs themselves, for washing. There was far too much laundry for me to manage in our tiny sink.

That morning, while sipping our deliciously thick brews, we learned a little something about one of our favorite coffee blends, Trung Nguyen no. 8. First, the coffee beans are fed to weasels. Then, days later, they are harvested from the weasel poo, ground up, and brewed.

A Day at the Races

We wanted to spend several days walking around Ho Chi Min City, but we were overwhelmed by how much there was to see and do. To clear our heads, we spent a day at the racetrack. It was great fun, despite a bit of confusion about whether our pamphlet was recording the weights of the horses or the tiny jockeys on their backs. Forty-four kilograms seemed just as possible for both.

As a team, we were uncommonly accurate at picking winners. Nathan picked the horses who looked like they were tweaking on drugs and I chose the horses that looked the most excited to run in a race. Those horses that fell into both categories were champions. This strategy yielded us a win on every bet we placed. It was a shame that our maximum bet of a hundred thousand dong didn't cover much more than beer and our entrance fees.

Kit Kat, Without the Break

One night in Ho Chi Min, Nathan had a craving for a late-night snack. He left our hotel room alone, at 9:45 p.m., to cross the street for a quick stop at a corner store. He bought himself a

Kit Kat, then walked back across the street. When he arrived at the hotel's front door, he discovered the chain-linked barricade being closed for the night. The same little old lady that had pulled us off of the street to stay in her hotel was standing in the gap, pulling with all of her strength. Nathan met her venomous glare. She stood four-feet tall and had her birdlike legs planted firmly across the narrow entrance. This woman had seen Nathan and I coming and going from the hotel for several days. She did our laundry. When Nathan signaled to her that he would like to enter the hotel, she stated coldly, "No rooms."

He raised an eyebrow, pointed up to the second floor and replied, "Uh. I stay here." This did nothing to persuade her. She worked to close the metal doors with more urgency. Thankfully, Nathan did not waste his window of opportunity. He slid into the hotel lobby, pushing the tiny woman gently but firmly out of the way. She quickly closed the front gate to prevent additional intruders, then shuffled to catch up with him. He climbed the stairs two at a time, hoping the old woman would give up. I heard him coming down the hall, flip flops urgently thwacking the floor. He was being chased by hissing whispers imploring him to leave the premises. He loudly called, "Hey Jenny, can you please open the door. *Now*." I obliged. The tiny woman followed him to the door and stood with hands on hips, glaring at us. I had no idea what was happening. I stood bewildered as Nathan's irritation grew. He explained firmly, "I stay here! I've been staying here for three days! You did my laundry!"

He deliberately closed the door in the woman's face and turned to me. "There is a very good chance the police will be here in a short time."

I couldn't control my laughter. I buried my face in a pillow and laughed until I cried. Nathan was a bit too flustered to appreciate the situation at first, but he eventually joined in. The poor ol' coot couldn't keep track of her rooms. We crossed our fingers that she would remember she could check our passports. The police did not show up, but after the incident, she kept a close eye on Nathan.

The day we said farewell to Ho Chi Min, the old crone extracted her revenge. To say that I endured her punishment with a cool head would be a lie. She had been defeated by Nathan once, and didn't intend to face him alone again. She sent her crook son to do her dirty bidding. He explained that we had stayed more nights than we thought. A ruse that might work on some tourists, but I managed to deflect this cheap maneuver calmly and quickly. I produced bus tickets that proved the date of our arrival. The worm regrouped with lightning speed, attacking from a new angle. He changed the nightly rate. It was at approximately this time that I began to unhinge. I walked up to the front of his crazy grannie's hotel, pulled a sign off of the wall with the price clearly written and walked back to hold it in front of his smug face. You might be asking yourself: Why didn't we just pay the agreed upon price and walk out?

The old shrew had our passports. We had no choice but to meet somewhere in the middle. Thank God Nathan remained calm. He paid the inflated rate and grabbed my arm to pull me out into the street. I was furious. An injustice such as this can ruin an entire day, sometimes longer. It jades all of your interactions for a period of time directly proportional to the sting of the swindle.

I was fuming as we walked away from the hotel. We needed a taxi to the bus station. The first taxi driver told us the bus station had moved eight miles out of town, and the ride would cost thirty dollars. The second taxi driver told us to forget the meter and bargain for a price. The third driver said it was fifteen miles and would cost forty dollars. When we informed him that we would take public transportation, he claimed that no bus route would take us there.

I couldn't contain myself. "Buses don't go to a *bus station*? Do you think I am going to believe such a *stupid* lie?" I rolled my eyes and scowled. Nathan got sympathetic looks from passersby. They seemed sad for him, that he would be burdened with a woman like me.

I growled my intention to walk. Fifteen miles, if need be, to the bus station. Nathan groaned. He walked with me just long enough to allow my anger to simmer, then suggested we try one last taxi. The man turned out to be an honest driver. For seven dollars, he delivered us to a bus leaving for My Tho, and we shuffled on board. We had learned from a helpful teenage girl in the bus station that the trip would cost us each two dollars and fifty cents. As soon as our bags were stowed in the very back of the bus, the money collector told us the price was fifteen dollars per person. Surprisingly, I had sufficiently recovered to play it cool. Nathan however, had reached the end of *his* patience. He started frantically crawling over seats, stacks of luggage, and other passengers toward the back of the bus, to get our bags. I got up, calmly stared the man in the eyes and told him that we would get off the bus if he didn't give us the right price. He lowered it to fifteen dollars for both of us. I turned, found an older gentleman sitting near us, and asked him how much one ticket was. He held up two dollars and fifty cents. By this time, Nathan was in a frenzy, hauling our things closer to the door. Just as he was about to throw them out into the street, the man took my five dollars and smiled. He waved at Nathan to sit back down.

We spent the first twenty minutes of the two-hour ride in silence. Nathan broke it with a confession. "If you hadn't been here, I would *never* have taken this bus. I would have gotten off no matter what, even after he gave the right price, and found another bus." I was surprised, though I understood his sentiment. We had both been stretched well past our limits. I made my own confession, "If you hadn't handled payment back at the hotel, I would have crumpled the sign with the price of a room into a ball and shoved it down that man's throat."

Mekong Delta

When we arrived in My Tho, we learned that the bus station was, unsurprisingly, two miles out of town. We needed to hire a moped taxi. I threatened to walk again, but Nathan was clearly not in the mood, so we agreed to a dollar for each of us. The journey from Ho Chi Min to My Tho would have cost fifteen dollars apiece, had we accepted our hotel's offer to deliver us in a luxury, air-conditioned van. Our way, it cost seven dollars apiece. I can see why people take the luxury option, but honestly, despite the frustration and the difficulties that come from doing it yourself, it is much more rewarding. At least, that's what we exceptional tourists tell ourselves when we recover from our blinding rage.

Truth is, we would have missed out on a dozen interactions with locals. Doing things the hard way gave us an opportunity to learn something about the people and the country we were exploring. It is important to keep in mind that in Vietnam, just like anywhere else on the planet, for every one crooked con-artist, there are thousands—maybe hundreds of helpful, sincere, and kind people.

Traveling through the Mekong Delta was a unique experience. Most of the cities within the region were unattractive. They were hubs of industry; their streets were cluttered with trash, rotting produce, and the inevitable grime left by heavy traffic. The Mekong ran through the heart of every city, carrying barges loaded with produce, mud for bricks, durian fruits, coconut husks for fuel, and of course, rice. Farmers used its tributaries to transport their goods for export. Outside of the cities, the Mekong Delta was beautiful. Rice paddies, sugar cane plantations, orchards, and gardens stretched for hundreds of miles. The land was green, and the sky was blue; nothing else existed. There was an oddly alluring loneliness to the countryside.

We spent more time in the Mekong Delta than most backpackers. From My Tho, we traveled to Ba Tri, then Vin

Long, another city on the water. There, we hired a man to take us on a boat tour and arrange a homestay for us with a local family. This was our first exposure to the homestay. The boat tour was rather terrible. In part, thanks to the company of the captain's young son, a boy of about fifteen with a number of severe personality disorders. He became fond of pretending to speak English using made up words to describe the things he saw around him. It might have been more tolerable, maybe even endearing, had I not gotten the distinct impression he was making fun of us. Besides his taunting, the boy tried, and succeeded, in capturing and kissing me with an open, drooling mouth. This incident amused Nathan immensely, especially since he was able to document it with our camera. The little rat had asked to pose for a picture with me, then pulled a fast one when the flash went off. Nathan is convinced that at some point in the future, I will be able to look at that picture and laugh. So far, every time I look at it, I want to punch something.

The homestay portion of the trip was excellent. We were delivered to the humble home of a middle-aged woman and her husband. She smiled kindly as she showed us a room where we could put our things. It was a private spot at the back of her compound with a mosquito net hanging over a double bed. A lock and key hung by the door for our security. She let us borrow bicycles to explore the narrow island paths that wound for miles in every direction. Before we left her home, she gave us a small piece of paper with something carefully written on it. When we looked questioningly at the note, she pointed at herself and the house behind her, then down at the paper. She smiled when comprehension dawned on our faces. She was giving us her address, in case we got lost. If it had been just me, I would have needed the address, but Nathan had no problem getting us back to her door. When we tired of the sun, we returned the bikes, plopped ourselves into hammocks and enjoyed cold tea, and plate after plate of fresh fruit as they were presented to us. The woman's husband strummed Motown classics on his guitar and tried to teach Nathan, who has played for years, a few chords. Nathan was a diligent student. He made his teacher proud by strumming a few songs of his own. The man returned a knowing wink and watched Nathan for a few minutes to pick up pointers.

We slept long and deep that night, and we woke feeling invigorated. We knew we were in for a challenging day, but for some reason, we were ready. We weren't anxious about the inevitable confusion of interpersonal communication, or long hours spent crammed uncomfortably in buses and boats. We were excited to prove ourselves as exceptional tourists.

The day began with a hearty homestay breakfast of eggs, fish, and rice. After breakfast, we walked a mile to the ferry landing. It was just loading as we arrived, so there was no waiting. We floated across the Mekong, then disembarked near a busy market, where we found a local bus to a town called Sa Dec. Sa Dec was not a town that tourists frequented. I wouldn't be surprised if we were the only tourists that had ever visited. We were dropped off in another crowded market and were instantly the center of attention. Children surrounded us. One snuck up beside Nathan and started sniffing him. They took pictures of us while their friends moved stealthily around behind us, to make it look like we were all hanging out.

From Sa Dec, we found a bus with the name of a river, one we were fairly certain we wanted to cross, on the front of it. When the bus pulled over, we boarded. It was full of teenage girls and elderly women, two demographics that love Nathan. He was surrounded by a cluster of giggling women who occasionally reached out to touch him. One surprisingly wily old woman managed to pick his pocket. She gave a toothless grin while she held up his wallet, to flaunt her success. I nodded my head at her, as if to show my respect for her cunning. She handed the wallet to me instead of back to Nathan, then loudly scolded him, while shaking a finger in his face, for being careless. This demonstration had everyone on the bus falling out of their seats with laughter.

The bus took us exactly where we hoped it would, to another ferry crossing. We boarded right away and found some upper deck seats. Seconds after sitting down, a man accosted us. He was wearing what looked like a police uniform, so we introduced ourselves cautiously. He turned out to be the ferry administrator, who spoke excellent English. He asked if we wanted to come up and see the captain's cabin. I couldn't help hearing my dark side whispering that he wanted to get us alone to bribe or trick us.

Instead, he brought us to the upper deck, where the captain's cabin was located. We talked for a few minutes about his rise to the position of administrator, then about his family, and then conversation shifted to the American War. He pulled up his pant leg to show us the terrible scar above his knee. It was caused by an American artillery shell explosion in his hut when he was a child. He shook his head in wonder. "Can you believe it was the American doctors who then saved my life?"

He told us that he didn't hold any grudges, that every American he had ever met had been friendly. When the ferry reached the opposite shore of the river, he disembarked with us and pointed us in the direction of the bus stop. We said goodbye with heartfelt handshakes and smiles. I felt guilty for thinking the worst and vowed to work harder at trusting people.

We walked several hundred feet to the bus stop but weren't sure what to look for. There was no way to tell how often buses came or where they went. An elderly woman with deep wrinkles at the corners of her eyes, took pity on us. She pulled me down beside her on a wooden bench. She spent a few seconds running her fingers through my frizzy curls, then we tried talking to each other. Neither of us could understand a single thing the other said. Thankfully, she found the process amusing, not frustrating. She motioned for us to do as she did, so we boarded a local bus at her heels. It brought us to the center of Long Xuyen.

We found a room and spent the remainder of the evening congratulating ourselves for our successful day of travel. Over the course of eight hours, we had taken two ferries, three buses, and paid just under two dollars each for the entire trip. We only met one man who spoke English. The rest of our communication had been without words. If we had booked this trip with a tourism agency, we would have paid over twenty dollars apiece and missed out on a full day of interacting with friendly, silly, and genuinely helpful people.

That night I slept deeply until about two in the morning. I was awakened by the sound of someone riffling through our packs. It was Nathan. I asked groggily, "What are you doing? It's the middle of the night."

He whispered back urgently, "We have an emergency!" Personally, I use the word *emergency* sparingly, so he had my full attention.

Thank God my adrenaline kicked in. Otherwise, we might never have located the dental floss he so desperately needed. Ask anyone, I appreciate diligent dental care, but this was well past even my hygiene standards.

Say What?

By this point in our journey, Nathan and I had begun to recognize differences in our understanding of interpersonal communications. More times than I could count, we had stood side by side while listening to someone using broken English to explain something. About thirty percent of the time, we reported having understood the same information. The other seventy percent of the time our accounts of the interaction differed.

Thankfully, the differences were usually minor. Variations commonly occurred in our understanding of how much something was going to cost or what time a bus left. However, one misunderstanding was so spectacularly outlandish that it left us both reeling.

We were talking to a man who had approached us on the streets of Long Xuyen. He was hoping to persuade us to take a trip with him. That much was undisputed. What followed was a description of what we could expect if we took him up on his offer. When he had finished selling the experience, he asked if we thought it sounded like a good trip. We both answered yes to this question, but we declined his offer to be our guide because we were leaving town the next day.

While discussing the interaction later, Nathan and I were startled to discover the following:

Nathan had heard, "If you come on the trip, I will let you try whiskey with a snake heart soaking in it."

I heard, "If you come with me, I will find a snake and kill it for you. Quickly, we will skin it while it hangs from a tree, by turning its skin inside out. Then, we will pull out its still-beating heart and eat it with some delicious local rice wine. It will make you stronger."

Nathan and I exchanged our interpretations with jaws dropped. I was incredulous. We had been talking to the man for at least two minutes, not mere seconds. I couldn't believe that Nathan had heard a single sentence from the man's mouth, not a word more. I stood, and still stand, firmly by my interpretation, but so does Nathan by his. We will never know for sure what really happened during that conversation. At least, that's what I tell Nathan. I know what happened. He had a hard time understanding the man's thick accent, so he stopped paying attention.

In addition to our listening skills, our overall awareness as travelers was changing. The excitement of being abroad was no longer enough, on its own, to bring us happiness. People think that being a traveler is an easy job, but once the charm of being away from your home wears off, you discover that good days require tremendous effort. Happiness requires attention. I don't mean to say that our lives were terribly difficult, but we did work tirelessly to expand our comfort zones and take more risks.

In the Mekong Delta, we spent two weeks moving from town to town. From Long Xuyen, we traveled north on the river to Chau Doc, then west to Ha Tien. All along the way, we visited local markets, rented mopeds to explore the countryside, and did things the hard way. We zigged and zagged our way across the entire delta without knowing exactly why we were doing it. We had traveled ourselves into a rut. In our minds, there was only one solution. We required a mandatory decompression on a tropical island, with good food, white sand beaches, quiet nights of star gazing, and whiskey sipping. Phu Quoc Island would be our last stop in Vietnam. An island retreat to regroup and prepare for Cambodia.

I was almost certain I had seen it all in Vietnam. Then, on an extremely crowded bus ride to the coast, I saw an eighty-year-old woman jump out of her window because there was no other way to get out. She folded herself in half, shouted, "Bà sẽ xuống tại!" and leapt into the street like a ninja. This was the highlight of the Mekong Delta, as far as I was concerned. Nathan was wedged between five other elderly women in front of me, so he missed the incident. He did notice the woman was gone a minute later and turned to ask, "Hey, did an elderly woman just jump out a window?"

"*Bà sẽ xuống tại!*"
"*Grandma will get off now!*"

I was certainly going to miss Vietnam. It had made an impression on me. It had changed me. At midnight, when the countrywide, atonal screaming ceased, I started to feel a void in the world where the din of karaoke should have been. Vietnam was an auditory assault. Mornings sometimes came with the raspy, choking cough of strangers regurgitating their bronchial tubes outside of our hotel room. If the hacking didn't wake us, the bicycles with ice boxes full of frozen treats, playing circus songs on loud speakers did. Car horns were much more entertaining than a simple honk. Most involved a fade-out doppler effect, to mimic the sound of zooming past at a hundred miles an hour, or an echo feature. People paid others to ride around on bikes and mopeds screaming advertisements to anyone who would listen. Traveling performers strapped amplifiers to their mopeds and sang for tips at restaurants. Music played in markets, on the streets, and in people's homes.

All the noise was so routine that I had become incapable of sleeping with ear plugs. When wearing them, the quiet was so distractingly empty that I couldn't stop thinking about it.

Phu Quoc seemed the perfect choice for making the transition from Vietnam to Cambodia a smooth one. Both countries claim the island. If they can't decide, surely it's an ideal place to ease out of one and into the other.

From the coastal town of Ha Tien, we took a ferry to Phu Quoc. When we arrived, we learned that we were thirty miles from town. Even by Vietnamese standards, this was an impressive new record for transit station distance from city center. The only way to get there was on a bus. A single bus was parked on the road, which meant that we were at a serious disadvantage. In the United States, how badly you need something does not always directly correlate to how much it will cost. A bottle of water is the same price, regardless of whether you are thirsty. In Vietnam, things are different. If you need a cookie to survive, and there are twenty million cookies at the corner store, one cookie will still cost you fifty-thousand dollars. Why? Because you are desperate.

Our bus ride from the middle of nowhere to the beach cost us as much as a plane ticket from Bangkok to northern Thailand. To the bus driver's credit, even locals were forced to pay inflated prices.

We spent the next five days unwinding on white sand beaches, drinking margaritas, eating our favorite Vietnamese dishes, and watching magical sunsets every night. I felt a little under the weather, so I napped often and ate well. I was reminded of our first two weeks in Thailand, and our vow not to become the kind of travelers who ate pizza, drank too much, and didn't want anything to do with cultural experiences. It dawned on me that there was a time and a place for everything. After spending two weeks immersed in the Mekong Delta, it was blissful to stare down at a medium pizza with actual pepperonis and eat every morsel with moans of rapture.

Phu Quoc wasn't perfect. Just like elsewhere in Vietnam, locals used the same aggravating tactics to empty our wallets. One evening, we tried renting a moped for an hour from our hotel. The going rate for moped rentals was five dollars for eight hours. Nathan approached the receptionist at our hotel and asked, "Could we rent a moped for one hour?"

The young man replied, "OK. Five dollars."

"Well, it's already four in the afternoon, so it's not a full day rental. Just one hour so that we can ride into town for dinner." Nathan replied.

"No, it's not."

Nathan pointed to the clock behind the man's head and asked, "No? It's not four in the afternoon?"

The receptionist shot back, "If you rent now, you keep for eight hours. Five dollars."

"We won't be needing the moped in the middle of the night. We just want it for the next hour."

"Five dollars."

"OK, no problem. We'll go rent one from the guy next door. Have a good afternoon."

Realizing he had lost the battle, the man sighed and said, "One dollar for one hour."

This is how it went with almost every transaction. Most of the time we didn't let it bother us. But sometimes, when one of us felt we needed to teach someone in the tourism industry a lesson, we would do what we did that evening. We walked to the shop next door even after we had gotten the price we wanted. Out of principle.

We made plans to cross into Cambodia on the back of moped taxis from Ha Tien. While we watched the sunset from our bungalow one last time, Nathan read up on our next destination. He learned that in Cambodia, you can pay to blow up a cow with a rocket launcher. Apparently, you buy the cow regardless of whether you hit it or not. This ensures the business makes a tidy profit while you enjoy the thrill of being a jackass.

As planned, the next day we sped from the ferry terminal in Ha Tien on the back of two moped taxis to the Prek-Chak border crossing. Our drivers wedged our packs between their legs on the front of the mopeds and made room for us on the seats behind them. Nathan's driver spoke English and was curious about our trip. My driver was not interested in or capable of conversation. When we reached Prek-Chak, our drivers informed us that they would cross the border without us. They promised to wait with our bags on the other side.

Our visas were issued with smiles, and we were sent to the shack next door for a health evaluation. The prospect of enduring any kind of medical scrutiny had me feeling nervous. I was still recovering from a nasty cough, and just thinking about it made my throat tickle. I knew I couldn't give in to the urge. I filled out a questionnaire that asked, in the last seven days have you:

1) Had a cough?
2) Had a sore throat?

3) Sneezed?
4) Had a fever?

    The truthful answer to every question, in my case, was yes. As I stared wide eyed at the tiny cement quarantine box, a medical professional eyed me suspiciously from behind his desk. The minutes dragged on and the tickle in my throat got stronger. I gave my healthiest smile, then checked *none of the above*. When we made it to our final passport check, I was rasping like a lifelong smoker, trying to keep the cough from giving me away. Thankfully, I didn't tip off the officials. I was free to contaminate the Cambodian countryside with Vietnamese germs. As promised, our drivers were waiting for us just past the Cambodian customs building.

Chapter Four

Cambodia
For the Exceptional Tourist, Khmer

Our moped taxis dropped us off in a town called Kep. It was a lazy town with little more to offer than fresh crab and a bus station. Nathan and I had no interest in seafood, so we spent a single night before heading along the coast to Kampot.

On our first morning in Kampot, I somehow managed to lock myself in our bathroom. The doorknob detached from the locking mechanism. Nathan's skillful wielding of a credit card eventually extricated me.

Most people might consider this kind of start to their day a bad omen. In my experience, there's no better way to start a morning than laughing/crying hysterically in a tiny room that smells like poop. It can only get better from there.

We rented a moped for the day, and despite being given some of the worst directions I have ever heard, we located a cave to explore. The directions went something like this:

Go five-and-a-half miles and take a left. You will see a tiny rhino statue in a field of rice. Continue three miles to a rock. At the tree that is bent, stay right. You will reach a six-way intersection. Follow the path with the deepest ditch, which should be the third to your left, until you reach a cave temple.

We did this without an odometer. There was no tiny rhino or bent tree as far as either of us could tell, and there were many rocks. There cave we found was also missing a temple. I'm not sure how Nathan did it. The road led us to an old quarry. When we arrived, a runner was sent to ask a man to stop blowing up sticks of dynamite long enough for us to explore. I turned to Nathan, "Seems safe to me. What could possibly go wrong in a dynamite riddled underground cavern? Let's do this!"

Five boys between the ages of twelve and twenty-nine escorted us into the blackness. The cave was one of my favorites.

Thick vines hung down to the dusty floor from natural chimneys reaching fifty feet to the jungle above. We used the vines and roots to swing into the dark from the tops of huge boulders. We climbed through tiny spaces, snaked our way deep into the side of the mountain, then drank blood from a monkey skull.

Fine, the blood drinking didn't happen, but it did feel an awful lot like we were hanging out in Indiana Jones's Temple of Doom.

Following the cave, we discovered another gem of Kampot, a privately owned zoo. It was the strangest, and in my opinion, one of the most dangerous things we did during our travels. Nathan's encounter with an escaped monkey while trying to hide a bunch of bananas behind his back was the least of my concerns. Besides being a zoo, the complex felt like the set of a horror movie. The grounds were silent except for the creaking of an abandoned Ferris wheel, rusted with age and slowly spinning in the wind. A child of eight was sleeping, or dead, in one of the seats suspended fifteen feet above the ground. As if the bizarre playground equipment weren't unnerving enough, the cages were riddled with rusty pockmarks from decades of neglect. Each was isolated from the others, and from anyone who might be able to help, should a door or tiny padlock fail.

I was anxious the moment we approached the lion cage. Rebar, brittle and twisted, and a miniature padlock were the only barrier between us and a visibly ravenous lioness. I'd had a stronger lock on my junior high gym locker, which had me on edge, because my gym locker had been repeatedly violated by adolescent weaklings.

Nathan, on the other hand, calmly chatted as I slowly backed away from the cage. The lioness paced back and forth, never taking her eyes off us. We had to walk fairly close to the cage to get by, and as we did, she made to attack. She lowered her head, locked her eyes on us and charged the side of the cage. *This* got Nathan's attention. We ran as fast as we could back to the main path. For those of you who have never been hunted by a two-hundred-and-fifty-pound cat, it is terrifying.

Apart from the terror, we both thoroughly enjoyed the experience. We watched the gibbons longest. They swung with silent fluidity, using all four of their long limbs. The graceful jungle creatures we had missed in Northern Laos fascinated us.

American Robots

Before checking out of our hotel in Kampot, we met another Norwegian. His name was Viggo, and he was obviously in distress. He approached us when he heard us organizing a van transport to Sihanookville. He had just come from Sihanookville and was very upset about having left something behind. He had been calling his hotel for hours, trying to determine whether they still had his items. He begged for our help. Nathan promised him that if we could help, we would. He asked Viggo what items he had left behind.

Viggo told us that he had forgotten a pair of hiking boots. He dismissively shook his head when I commiserated that hiking boots were a terrible loss. He clarified, "No, the boots I don't care about. There is a tube of cream inside one of the boots. It is *irreplaceable*. It is medicine that I *need*."

With that, we agreed to ask around when we got there. Viggo was grateful. I asked him how he would get his medicine from us, after we had retrieved it. He must have also been eavesdropping on our morning conversation because he knew we were heading to Phnom Penh after Sihanookville. He intended to wait for us there. He gave us his contact information and shook our hands enthusiastically. We left for Sihanookville thirty minutes later.

Nathan refused to pronounce the word Sihanookville correctly. He referred to it as Snooky, Snookville, and Snatty. I'm not sure why it drove me crazy at the time, but it did. I took it upon myself to correct him every time, which in hindsight is probably why he did it.

Our first item of business in Sihanookville was to check on Viggo's boots and his irreplaceable medicine. We found his hotel and went inside to speak with the owner, a British man covered in tattoos. When we explained our purpose, the British man brightened, "Oh, that bloke has been calling for the last two days about his damned boots. We told him that they were still here, but he never came. I am happy to give them to you, if that will make him stop calling."

Viggo was telling the truth about his boots not being worth the trip. They were falling apart and smelled as if they had walked the earth three times over. I couldn't resist looking inside, to see whether Viggo's medicine was still there. What I found was unexpected.

I had assumed that Viggo's medicine was something from his own country. An item that would be impossible to find anywhere else, and one that he desperately needed. Instead, I found a tube of generic antibiotic ointment. It didn't make sense. Antibiotic ointment was available everywhere. In Cambodia, it cost less than fifty cents for a tube.

I didn't investigate further. Nathan and I packed Viggo's things into a plastic bag, and hauled them around for the next several days, waiting to meet up with him. If Viggo's tube of ointment was more than it seemed, neither of us wanted to know about it.

Sihanookville was a town where backpackers went, and presumably still go, to waste their lives. Local bars and restaurants offer free room and board to backpackers willing to work as servers and bartenders. The prospect of living and working in a booze-induced stupor while incurring no expenses other than the drugs, extra booze, and visa extensions, apparently appeals to people. We didn't stay long.

On the bus ride to Phnom Penh, Nathan informed me out of the blue, that my deepest desire might be realized before the day was out. Naturally, I was thrilled. Then I wondered how he knew my deepest desire. "Wait. What's my deepest desire again?" I asked.

"I ate something bad. My stomach is rumbling. We're stuck on a bus for six hours without a bathroom. I might poop my pants." He groaned.

This caught me off guard. "Ew. What? You thought I *wanted* you to lose control of your bowels? I was just laughing at the possibility. I never wished it upon you." He gave me a good long look, then nodded his head slowly, as if still trying to decide how honest I was being.

I'm not sure what it says about a woman when her boyfriend believes her greatest wish is to see him poop in his pants. Somehow, I unintentionally gave Nathan this impression. Perhaps my enthusiasm when informing him of the possibility of such an event had been misleading.

We both went back to reading our books, hoping for a quick and painless journey.

That night, our first in Phnom Penh, Nathan waited for Viggo in our hotel room while I went in search of dinner. I decided on cheese and crackers, something simple and cheap. Sometimes it can be difficult to find cheese in countries like Cambodia. In countries where it's hot, electricity is scarce, and a respect for the beauty of a good block of cheese is lacking, there is a solution: the savior of many a tourist, Vache Qui Rit. In English, Laughing Cow Cheese. It's a spreadable, heat resistant, non-refrigerated cheese.

In Southeast Asia, it is often the only cheese within hundreds of miles. I walked into a shop with an assortment of items hanging from walls, stacked in cabinets and hidden in drawers. A woman about my age was behind a glass case, which held some of the store's most expensive items. I didn't see cheese, so I asked, "Do you have any Vache Qui Rit?"

The woman smiled and nodded while unlocking her glass case to dig around. She pulled out a pack of batteries. I chuckled. I hadn't realized how similar the words, *Vache Qui Rit* and *batteries* sounded. I shook my head to indicate that they weren't what I had been looking for, then tried again in English, "Cheese?"

She stared blankly at me for a moment, then shook the pack of batteries above her head and assured me, in her own language, that this was indeed what I was asking for. I tried again with the age-old tactic of speaking very slowly and *very loudly*. I thought the words Vache Qui Rit might be easier to understand if I also included a performance, so I mimed my intent to eat it. This had her wide eyed and speechless. She decided to phone a friend for clarification. While looking at me, she repeated the word *battery* into the phone. She got the answer she had expected, confirmation that the tourist wanted to eat batteries. She started laughing, then she pretended to eat the batteries while maintaining eye contact with me. I didn't have it in me to spoil the moment, so I eyed the batteries she was holding up as though I was considering whether they were the right ones. Then I said with regret, "No. Too small." I mimed eating much larger batteries before walking back to the hotel.

I was pleased to have represented Americans as battery-powered robots. It didn't seem that far from the truth.

All in a day's work.

When I got back to the hotel room, Viggo was there talking with Nathan. He was thrilled to have his boots and his antibiotic ointment. We didn't let on that we had searched the boot. He pulled a bag of Sri Lankan coffee from his pack and handed it to us. "As a thank you. Please, take my gift. I was in Sri Lanka before Cambodia."

We didn't argue. The coffee was obviously of high quality. I was relieved to see Viggo depart with his belongings. The exchange never made sense to me. Norwegians.

Dark Past

    We spent our first day in Phnom Penh exploring on foot, visiting temples, the National Library, the Royal Palace, and the impressive Central Market. Nathan kept insisting that if we stopped by the U.S. Embassy we would be invited in for drinks and snacks. I don't know where he got the impression that Embassies were like fraternities, but I didn't have the heart to tell him otherwise. We passed a row of large trees at the outskirts of Wat Phnom, a mountain temple jutting from the center of a city block. Dozens of monkeys hung from their branches, hooting and screeching to visitors as they passed. I walked up to a girl and her brother, who were clearly about to do something stupid. I put my hand on the girl's arm and gave a bit of unsolicited advice. "Are you aware that the monkey about to come down here and grab your banana could rip your face off in about 1.5 seconds? Please be careful. I can't stick around to watch this."

    My words surprisingly did not have the desired effect. The clueless girl giggled, then handed her brother the banana. I made eye contact with Nathan as we walked away. He whispered in a sad voice, "Can't win them all."

    When we started to delve a little deeper into the history of Cambodia, our mood changed drastically. It is a country with a devastating past; a past I knew embarrassingly little about. My knowledge of the Khmer Rouge was limited to the name. I didn't know anything about the atrocities Pol Pot and his followers committed against the Khmer people. The name Pol Pot conjured vague sympathy for the distant troubles of a foreign nation.

    Nathan and I spent three days walking through the terrible past. At the Genocide Museum, we looked at thousands of pictures of the innocent faces of men, women, and children, all murdered. We walked through the Killing Fields trying to understand the crimes of Cambodia's leaders. We wanted to learn as much about the reign of the Khmer Rouge as we could, to honor the lives of its victims. The Cambodian people do not shy away from their history. They have created museums, monuments, written books, and made movies to shed light on their troubled past. They are a nation trying to heal, trying to ensure the mistakes of the past are not repeated.

We left Phnom Penh with heavy hearts, and waning motivation to continue exploring. It took time for us to process all that we had learned. We made a conscious choice to focus on the amazing recovery of the Khmer people, rather than their terrible past. We wanted to meet the genocide survivors. We wanted to celebrate their strength and make a sincere effort to get to know as many Cambodians as we could. We decided to work harder as travelers, to do more than visit a list of tourist destinations in our guidebook.

We headed north, in search of something new. Our first stop was Kratie. The bus ride took almost eight hours with a bathroom stop about halfway. I realized, with a jolt, how ambivalent I had become when a woman elbowed me out of the way as she stole the bathroom stall for which I had been waiting fifteen minutes. I caught myself returning her smile as she closed the door in my face. Maybe I was finally fitting in.

On the way back to the bus, I caught sight of a gigantic pile of tarantulas in a basket by the side of the road. A woman had spiced them, presumably cooked them, though I did not get confirmation, and was selling them for twenty-five cents apiece. Of course, I bought one. I had a difficult time opening the plastic bag it was in, and an even a harder time forcing myself to touch it.

Nathan was not filled with admiration at my bold risk taking. I caught him looking around for another free seat. I stared down at the hairy beast in the palm of my hand, half expecting it to come back to life and jump at my face. I looked my fear in its many eyes, then I ate it. I couldn't bring myself to eat the belly.

Who would want to eat partially digested bug parts inside a bug part?

It wasn't bad. It wasn't good either. I had no idea how difficult it would be to eat a tarantula. I'm afraid of clowns too, and I honestly think it might have been easier to eat a clown.

It didn't hit me until I was lying in our hotel room that night, trying to fall asleep. Where had all of those spiders come from? The old woman selling them had been feeble. There was no way she could have captured *that* many if they were difficult to find. Had we just entered the most densely populated spider territory in the world?

Ferry ≠ Canoe

In Kratie, we rented a moped to drive north along the river. We had heard there was a ferry crossing to the largest Cambodian island in the Mekong. However, we did not know the name of the island, which would have been helpful. We rolled into Sambour, the town with the alleged ferry and started asking questions. In truth, *asking questions* isn't an accurate description of what I had to do. I was reduced to using a cigarette ad as a visual aid to point at a sailboat. For some reason, I thought it would be helpful to mimic waves with my arms by slithering them up and down, then left and right. From the way people responded, I realized that some were concerned I was having a seizure.

Finally, a man took pity on me. He broke up the mob of giggling adolescents and concerned adults and indicated that I could relax my arms. He pointed to the left. Apparently, my sign language wasn't confusing to *all* Cambodians. We drove to the left.

The scene repeated itself.

There was no boat. I did my best, again, to find out where the boat was. I was surrounded by a new crowd of cheerful and confused people. My gesturing became more frantic, making my frustration apparent, which caused one young girl to scream and ran away. At this, an older woman pointed to the right. It was hard to say whether she was trying to get rid of us or she knew what we were looking for. We drove right.

The scene repeated itself.

I was at the absolute limit of my patience. I whined, "Nathan, there is no ferry. I look like I'm suffering from a neurological disorder out here."

Just as I was climbing back onto the bike, a woman who understood some English and who probably felt bad for the idiots driving back and forth from one end of town to the other, approached. She told us to stop in the market and ask for a "touk," which is the Khmer word for boat.

Nathan squeezed my leg affectionately while I got situated behind him. He looked at me over his shoulder, "You look adorable miming waves."

I reluctantly used our new vocabulary word on the street across from the market. A man jumped from his chair, grabbed our arms and dragged us down a narrow alley to the riverside. Another man was waiting there with a tiny canoe. It resembled a ferry only in that it could float on water. We negotiated for about ten minutes, but for the first nine of those minutes, we had no idea what was happening. From his irritated grunting, the canoe owner was clearly annoyed that we didn't know the name of the place we were going. We were annoyed by this as well. We couldn't understand why our emphatic pointing toward the island, which was visibly located less than half a mile away was not enough to make our plans obvious. We gave up, resigned to go with whatever happened and pay whatever price. An eight-year-old girl with a shy smile crept up and tapped the man, most likely her father, on the shoulder. He bent down and let her whisper something into his ear. With a nod of encouragement to her, the man stepped back. She explained in her tiny voice that the island with homestays was called Koh Rougniv. Her father couldn't get his boat all the way to the village, but he could deliver us to a beach ten miles from it. It would cost five dollars.

I wanted to put the little girl in my backpack and keep her as a translator. I gave her a round of applause and told her that she was twice as smart as me because she knew Vietnamese and English, which made her giggle. When her father saw our smiles and nods of understanding, he patted her on the head and sent her skipping back to the busy market. Nathan helped him roll the bike to the water's edge, where they both strained to lift it into the bobbing canoe. The boat swayed awkwardly with its new cargo. I chuckled to myself at the risks we were taking with a moped we had rented for seven dollars. If the owner of that bike had known what we were planning, it is unlikely he would have agreed to our overnight rental.

We traversed the Mekong on a wobbly, eight-foot canoe, without incident. The man helped unloaded the bike, then Nathan drove it sputtering and spinning up a sand dune to the dirt path above. It was afternoon and the clock was ticking for us to find someone to take us in for the night.

I hopped on the back of the moped, and we sped off into the heart of the island. There were no roads, just foot paths barely wide enough for a single moped, and by the look of them, most had never seen one. They were a tangled mesh, meandering through fields of rice and sparsely wooded areas. Nathan had a great time navigating the tight curves, zipping over boards that crossed small streams, and pushing our rental moped to its limits. I enjoyed the scenery, but not the feeling that we were wandering farther and farther from food and shelter.

I saw the stump several seconds before Nathan slammed into it, so I had time to brace myself. He had seen it too and tried to swerve past it but hadn't been able to miss it entirely. One of the foot pegs took the brunt of the force. It was bent in such a way as to make shifting impossible. The bike stalled. I tried mightily to avoid scolding Nathan for driving like a maniac through the woods on a rental moped. If Nathan noticed my irritation, he didn't acknowledge it. Instead, he calmly took stock and said, "Well, I think we got lucky."

I raised an eyebrow, "I'm not sure we agree on the meaning of the word lucky."

"Well, it could be worse. We're stuck in second gear. We can still drive the moped, if it starts."

Miraculously, it did start, and since we didn't have the tools to fix it, we made our way slowly back to a path that appeared heavily traveled. We hoped to stumble into the town we knew was located somewhere nearby. About thirty minutes later we started seeing stilt houses that had signs reading "homestay" on their gates. We struck a deal with a plump woman who neither spoke nor understood a single English word. Her round face was flushed pink with embarrassment as we tried to communicate. Her shiny black hair hung loosely around her shoulders and her features were soft and motherly. She rubbed her hands together nervously as she concentrated on our efforts to arrange meals and a bed. I'm not sure how we managed to convey our intention to pay three dollars each, to spend the night on her floor, but we did. Once the formalities were out of the way, she relaxed, introducing herself as Chenda. We thanked her, dropped our belongings in her stilt house, then headed out for a walk. She signaled for us to be back for dinner, before the sun went down, then trotted off to gather ingredients.

There were dozens of kids in the village, all screaming hellos and goodbyes at the top of their lungs. Most weren't sure which was the appropriate greeting, so yelled both. "Hello. Goodbye! Hello. Goodbye!"

I bought candy at a small shop, but despite my relentless attempts to get close enough to hand it out, no one seemed interested. I was disappointed, but also impressed that the lesson about not taking candy from strangers had made it all the way to rural Cambodia. Either that, or there is something universally disturbing about someone giving sweets to children. I gave up and resigned myself to watching the kids watch us. Every so often, I jumped up to give chase, causing them to howl with hysterical laughter as they scattered in mock terror. After tiring myself out with this game, I plopped down on the steps of our stilt house, panting. A man approached, walking quickly on the narrow path, carrying a pile of books in his arms. He yelled a greeting when he caught our attention. Word had gotten out on the island that there were two Americans staying in a stilt house. He introduced himself as Samnang, an entrepreneur who was working to promote the island's homestay program. He had several books with pictures and questions written in both English and Khmer. They were tools he shared with all visitors to help them get to know their hosts. Chenda was relieved to have a better way to communicate with us.

That evening, after we had eaten the delicious dinner she prepared, we sat with her and several of her friends. I poured Nathan and myself a couple glasses of water from a pitcher she had filled for us. I took a sip while the women watched me with strange, expectant looks on their faces. The water was hot and soapy. I quickly motioned to Nathan that he should put the glass down, and sputtered, "Don't drink the water!"

He looked from my grimace to the wide-eyed faces staring at us, "Why?"

"They put it there for us to wash our hands. It's fifty percent dish soap. Ugh, terrible."

Nathan laughed, then the women all started to laugh. The incident helped us remember not to take ourselves too seriously, and it served as a perfect ice breaker.

We spent the next three hours huddled over books. The women wanted to know if we had siblings and if so, how many, and what were their names and their ages. They wanted to know where we were from, how we said our names, and how we wrote them. More than anything else, they wanted to teach us their language, Khmer. They wanted to share their lives with us. When we showed curiosity by asking questions, or trying to repeat the words they said, they were thrilled. They laughed and hugged us like we were dear friends. They shared their own family trees, pointing at pictures that hung from the stilt house walls. They quizzed us on the pronunciation of useful English phrases, then made sure we knew them in Khmer.

When we finally said goodnight, we felt as if we had made real friends. The villagers had sincerely opened their hearts to us. We hadn't been simply a means to income; we had been guests. It was refreshing, and for us, very new.

The next morning, we had a quick breakfast of rice and vegetables before saying goodbye. As we rode our damaged moped back toward the boat landing, children ran behind screaming, "Hello. Goodbye! Hello. Goodbye!"

Several hundred feet past the steep embankment where we had been dropped off the day before, we noticed a small shop. The man working there waved at us and shouted an English greeting. We were surprised but pleased that we might have found someone who could tell us where the real ferry landing was located.

We approached the shop in second gear, slowing to say hello. The young man stepped from the building and waited in the grass beside the path. His short, black hair was parted on the side and combed carefully at his temples. He would have looked like a businessman had he not been wearing torn jeans and a grease-stained button-up shirt. He was in his mid-twenties, judging by his demeanor and youthful complexion. Lean muscle covered his small frame, likely the product of years of manual labor. He noticed our bent foot pedal and jammed clutch, then motioned for us to get off the bike. "What happened?" He asked as he pointed.

"We hit a stump," Nathan explained, "and now we're stuck in second gear. It's a rental, so we need to get it fixed."

The man chuckled, "Ah, I see. It might be better to fix here, instead of letting the owner see?"

We both smiled sheepishly. Nathan offered, "That might be best."

"My name is Keo. I think I can help you. I have some tools."

Keo stepped into the shop and came returned with a sledgehammer. I looked at Nathan nervously. A sledgehammer?

I closed my eyes as Keo started pounding on our rental moped. When I peeked seconds later, he had straightened the peg, and the bike was able to shift like nothing had ever happened.

Keo grinned broadly and offered his hand to me, then to Nathan. "Happy to help. Where do you go?" He asked.

Nathan laughed, relieved that the damage from his bike stunt had been fixed so easily. "We're trying to find a ferry. Do you know where it is?"

"Yes! Keep going on this road. All the way until it hits the water. The ferry comes every thirty minutes. Sometimes longer."

We both shook Keo's hand a second time and thanked him for all of his help. He seemed pleased that he had been able to do so. We offered to compensate him for his time, but he refused to consider it.

We found the ferry landing without much trouble, then waited almost three hours for its arrival. When it finally did show up, Nathan said, "It comes every thirty minutes. Sometimes longer."

We Peddled, Then We Peddled

The success of our homestay on Koh Rougniv convinced us that we were on the right path. We needed more adventure, greater risk, and more interactions with the people of Cambodia. We traveled even farther north to a town called Stung Treng, where we began preparations for the adventure of a lifetime.

We found an outdoor equipment rental shop run by a man named Minh. When he learned that we were hoping to organize an excursion, he tried persuading us to join him on a two-day kayaking adventure. Two days on the river didn't appeal to us as much as a bicycle trip, so we decided to rent mountain bikes instead. It took a day to figure out how far we wanted to go and for how long we wanted the bikes, but when we did, Minh was as excited as we were. Our final destination lay 280 miles away, across poorly charted territory, through northern Cambodia. We planned to ride our bicycles to Siem Reap.

We packed small waterproof bags with rain gear, a change of clothes, flashlights, water bottles, and enough food for a single day. Each day on the road would require between thirty and seventy miles of riding. We didn't know where we would sleep or eat, the condition of the roads, or the weather forecast. For some reason, we weren't scared out of our minds. I don't know how we could have considered ourselves fit, having done almost no physical exercise for months, but we did. It was probably a good thing that we approached this trip with uninformed optimism. If we had understood the true nature of the undertaking, we would never have done it.

Minh insisted that we pick up our bikes from his office at dawn, on the morning of our departure. He offered to show us to the ferry and provide us with any last-minute supplies we might need. The map he gave us was terribly outdated, but he drew in pencil where he believed the new roads could be found. Just as in Vietnam, maps were a highly coveted item in Cambodia, rarely shared with outsiders. We were lucky to have one at all. The plan for our first day was to ride north to the border of Laos and Cambodia, about fifty-six miles away.

As requested, we met Minh at just past five in the morning at his shop. He rode with us to the ferry and took a few pictures to share with future, potential customers. Our arrangement was ideal. He had our large packs and our passports, and promised to transport them to Siem Reap, where he would wait for our arrival. When we safely returned his bikes to him, he would return our bags and passports to us.

Perhaps our time in Thailand without the comfort of our passports had softened us, softened our brains. It didn't occur to us until several days later that we had given up every item of worth to us, as insurance for Minh. The farther we got from Stung Treng, the more concerned I became about Minh's trustworthiness. I imagined him sneaking through customs at

JFK International Airport disguised as me. My father would probably appreciate his ingenuity and accept him into the family.

By the time the sun peeked over the tree tops that first morning, Minh was gone. Unfortunately, our timeliness was irrelevant. The ferry didn't leave for two hours. We stood with our bikes until just past seven, watching locals pour in from villages all along the Mekong, to sell their goods at the Stung Treng market.

When we finally reached the far shore, we hopped on our bikes and began to peddle. It took about five minutes for me to realize that I was *not* fit. It took ten minutes for me to admit to Nathan that we might be in some trouble, because I was exhausted. We both had a good laugh, then kept peddling. There was no turning back.

After an hour of riding through the jungle on a deserted gravel road, crossing numerous bridges constructed of rough-cut logs, without railings, Nathan made a rule. No wrecking on bridges. It seemed a wise rule. We were miles from the nearest human beings and hundreds of miles from the nearest medical facility.

It couldn't have been more than twenty minutes after this rule had been verbalized and agreed upon that I wrecked on a bridge. Bridge seems a crude descriptor and somewhat inaccurate. The structures were wooden planks or half logs propped over ditches and rivers. They were always uneven and always at the base of a steep hill. Nathan's handling of river crossings gave me false confidence. He rode ahead of me, traversing with ease. I approached at a similar speed and discovered much too late that I didn't have the skill or balance to handle the uneven boards. Halfway across the bridge my back tire slipped out from under me. To avoid being thrown from the edge, down to the rocky riverbed below, I pitched myself headfirst into the uneven logs at the center. Nathan turned to find me face down with my bike on top of me. When he came scrambling up to me, panic stricken, I tried to comfort him with a phrase he had used on me after crashing our moped on Koh Rougniv. "Well, I think I was lucky."

He rolled his eyes, then sighed with relief. "I think you were right. We might have different definitions of the word lucky."

I *had* been lucky. I survived a bike crash in the middle of the jungle with little more than a severely dented helmet and some raw spots to show for it. Nathan was shaken.

I smiled at him, then gave my best mock-look of irritation. "Would you quit making things look easier than they are!"

"I didn't know you were going to do exactly what I did. Are you crazy?" He shook his head disapprovingly.

"Listen, it all happened so fast. I thought I should try to keep up with you. Now I know. I have terrible balance on a bike while traversing round logs suspended twenty feet above the ground. Let's eat a snack. Adrenaline makes me hungry."

Nathan didn't bother with the snack. Instead, he found his pouch of bandages and antibiotic ointment. While I loudly crunched on my apple, he prodded my wounds to test their severity, then covered the most grievous with our best gauze. When he finished, I thanked him, kissed him on the cheek and promised to be more careful.

We got back on our bikes and began to peddle. The road was flat. The gravel was red. We peddled. Jungle stretched out to the horizon in both directions. We peddled. The sun grew hotter; sweat soaked through our clothes. We peddled. We rode for five hours; our muscles were reaching their limit. We had agreed to push ourselves hard until we found the waterfall Minh told us was along our route. Just after one in the afternoon, we saw a sign for it. An arrow pointed us down a narrow gravel road into the trees. We assumed the waterfall wasn't far, so we decided to eat our lunch in its mist.

We were in no condition to be observant or make intelligent decisions. It was over a 100 degrees, our water bottles needed refilling, and we had burned more calories than we had eaten in the last three days. If we had looked a little more closely at the sign that pointed toward the waterfall, we would have noticed the number ten followed by the letters *km* printed in the lower right corner. Ten kilometers might not seem far, a mere six miles, but it took us another forty-five minutes to reach the waterfall. Forty-five minutes of biking that was not in the direction of our final destination. When we reached the falls, we were the living dead; we walked with stiff limbs and glazed eyes to the water's edge.

We ate our lunch without joy, staring at the Mekong as it crashed over ledges and forced its way through rock formations. It marked the boundary between Laos and Cambodia. The enormity of the waterfall did not impress us as much as the enormity of the task ahead.

While stuffing our faces with tasteless calories, Nathan and I realized we had neglected to get the name of a place we could sleep. Minh had mentioned a guesthouse somewhere within a day's ride, but neither of us could remember where it was. We were too exhausted to spend precious energy worrying, so we got back on our bikes and peddled. When we finally reached the main road again, the benefit our muscles had received from a lunch break had long expired. We rode in silence.

Like a mirage, a single road sign rose from the red dust with what we hoped was the name of the village we sought. Our moods brightened. We turned off the road and followed the picturesque dirt path to a small village surrounded by thriving rice fields and grazing water buffalo. A soft breeze cooled the backs of our necks. We would have asked for help or directions, had we seen a single human being in that village, but we didn't. It was like riding through a *Twilight Zone* episode. It might have been paradise, had we not felt a thousand eyes watching our every move from behind closed doors and shuttered windows. The eerie silence gave us goose bumps. The echo of our whispers seemed to amplify, not dissipate. Five minutes in that village charged our legs with enough energy to get us the heck out.

On the main road, our nervous chatter kept us distracted until we reached an intersection. Our pencil-drawn map didn't show an intersection. Thankfully, a small shop on the corner had several patrons milling around. They all stared as Nathan and I got off of our bikes to point in opposite directions, each making a case. I never have an actual case when I argue for a particular direction. I just like to make sure that Nathan does.

Before we had the opportunity to reach a conclusion on our own, an old man walked three steps closer. It was getting late, and we needed shelter and food. I used sign language to indicate sleeping and eating, then pointed in both directions. The man caught my meaning. He said the name of a town, which left our brains as quickly as it entered, then pointed the way. We smiled our thanks and hopped back onto our bikes.

We peddled.

Twenty minutes later we were sure we had reached our destination. We rolled into a vast gravel lot. There were several cement structures, reminiscent of military barracks, located several hundred feet from the road. It seemed primitive but acceptable. We were in no position to be picky. A man came running out of one of the buildings waving his arms to get our attention. A good sign we thought.

Not so.

He was a military officer urging us in what I am certain was strong language, to get off of the property. He had a large gun strapped to his belt and his hand was resting on it as he ran. We had apparently stumbled into an embarrassingly poor "secure" border crossing station, a crossing closed to foreigners. I tried to calm the man down and simultaneously get information on a place to sleep. Nathan was only interested in trying to communicate our intent to leave.

When we were out of earshot, Nathan asked, "Did you notice the gun *this* time?"

I nodded, "Yeah. This time, I did notice the gun. He didn't have a friendly smile at all."

It was nearing dark, our water was running low, we hadn't eaten in hours, and there were dark clouds on the horizon. If I had been thinking clearly, I might have been more distressed. As it was, I insisted that we stop and ask everyone we saw about a guesthouse. This included water buffalo. The strategy ultimately paid off.

We ended up in a commune called Kampong Sra Loa on the Laos border. It was home to the only guesthouse within fifty miles. We were shown to a tiny room that could have passed for an oven, had it not come equipped with a bathroom sink and a hole in the floor. It was dark, stuffy, and absent of a mosquito net. I dropped my pack on the floor and peeled my sweaty, dirt-caked biking shorts down my legs. Every inch of skin that had been beneath them was covered in reddish-purple welts. It was the final straw.

Not only was I covered in heat rash, hungry, thirsty, and exhausted, I was also unbelievably sore. It hadn't even occurred to me that wedging a tiny metal bike-seat beneath me for ten hours might get uncomfortable. I was several orders of magnitude past uncomfortable. I whimpered when I sat, walked bow legged, and was more than happy to forgo the formality of a toilet seat. The pain was unlike anything I had ever experienced. I didn't know how I would get back onto the seat in the morning. Tears came to my eyes with the thought of another day of riding. I begged Nathan to come up with something to save me.

"You're a scientist. Invent something. I can't get back on my bike tomorrow. I can barely sit on a bed. What am I going to do?"

He chuckled so calmly I could have choked him. "Yeah, my butt hurts too. Ha."

I shot to my feet and screamed, "This isn't a *joke*! I feel nothing but despair. I hurt. Dammit, look at my legs! I'm covered in welts. The only way to get out of this misery is to sit myself on an iron bike seat that's about as comfortable as a *sledgehammer!*"

He gazed steadily and seriously into my eyes. "Your seat isn't made out of iron. That's ridiculous. Do you know how heavy your bike would be?"

I gazed steadily back, until neither one of us could keep a straight face. We both burst out laughing. How absolutely ridiculous the entire trip was! We weren't prepared for any of it. Our laughter helped ease the panic long enough for us to get cleaned up. Instead of collapsing into the bed, which was what I wanted to do, we accepted a dinner invitation from the proprietor.

We sat on the dining room floor, where the woman who ran the guesthouse had placed two large bowls of food. She had a son named Trong Tri who spoke excellent English. He worked for the Department of Agriculture and was home on vacation to see his closest friends and family. Along with inviting us to eat with him, he invited several of his childhood friends, Mr. Pon, Mr. Kung, and Chin-Chin. The women and children of the household sat at one bowl while Nathan and I sat at the other with the men. It was the first time we had been in a situation with people our own age, with a translator to help grease the communication wheels. Trong Tri's friends were just as eager to hear about us and our lives as we were to hear about theirs. They were all teachers at the local primary school.

We told them what we were planning for the next week and explained how we intended to make our way to Siem Reap through the jungle. Trong Tri stopped us and asked, "Where will you go tomorrow?"

Nathan answered, "Tomorrow we're riding to Chepp. We were told there was another guesthouse there."

Trong Tri's brow wrinkled thoughtfully. "No. There's no guesthouse. Also, the road might be impassable."

This wasn't good news. He must have sensed concern in the look that Nathan and I exchanged, because he quickly chimed in, "But, I know a man named Xuan Youthara who lives there. I can call him to see if he will let you sleep at his house."

Trong Tri did just that. He arranged for us to stay with Xuan when we arrived in Chepp. We didn't have Xuan's address, but we figured that Chepp couldn't be that big, and with his name and phone number we could find him. We spent the rest of the evening in a lighter mood, amazed at our luck in finding the one person in Kampong Sra Loa who could help us.

We learned a bit about the lives of our dinner mates. Mr. Pon was engaged to a sixteen-year-old student, whose parents were thrilled. They couldn't have asked for a more promising future for their daughter. A husband with a steady income was a rare thing. Mr. Kung was on the prowl for a young Cambodian girl similar to Pon's. It was difficult to determine whether Chin Chin was looking for or already had a wife. He was too happily drunk to do more than tell us that he loved us.

I called it a night much earlier than Nathan. From our room, I could hear the men asking him about our relationship, how we had met, when we would marry, and when we would have kids. Unfortunately, Nathan's considerately quiet answers made eavesdropping impossible. I had been wondering some of the same things. While they peppered Nathan with questions, they kept his glass full of Beer Laos.

He stumbled into the room just past one in the morning. Drunk. I had been trying to sleep, unsuccessfully, for several hours by that time, and had waning patience for his exhilarated rambling. I tried to share in his excitement at having such a wonderful evening while also trying to bring him gently down from his cultural-exchange high. Nothing was going to change our early morning departure. My alarm was set for five, and time to sleep was running short.

Nathan passed out on the bed next to me from exhaustion and probably dehydration on. In hindsight, he may have had the better approach. I was sober, hydrated, and squirming in the stifling heat of our room. With no fan, the air pressed down on my chest like a hot iron. If the heat hadn't kept me awake, the cockroaches would have. I lay sprawled on my back, flashlight at the ready, waiting to catch bugs and rodents in the act of violating my space. Nathan's peaceful countenance didn't even twitch when my flailing and swatting sent creatures scurrying to his side of the bed.

Toilet or Garden?

    I watched my clock all night. Just before five I got out of bed and started packing my things. Nathan woke to the rustling. I can't say I envied him. He had managed to sleep for several hours but looked much worse than I did. We were about to embark on our second day of biking on difficult roads, with limited sustenance, bruised posteriors, and in every possible way we were worse for wear. Our food supply was a bag full of individually wrapped kids snacks because we hadn't been able to find better supplies in Kampong Sra Loa. There were shrimp-flavored potato chips, muffins, and crackers. Even the cookies were shrimp flavored. Each awful item contained about fifty calories and was borderline inedible. Thankfully, we were smart enough to fill all of our water bottles.

    We were not in the mood or condition to face a tough day but didn't have much of a choice. Nathan pulled through with a bike-seat adaptation to protect my throbbing backside. He wrapped one of his long-sleeved shirts over the sledgehammer and tied it securely. I did my part by taking a handful of pain killers to dull the ache. By six, we were on the road.

    By six fifteen, we needed to stop and ask for directions. Our pencil-drawn map hadn't shown an intersection anywhere near Kampong Sra Loa, yet there we were, at a five-way intersection, not a sign in sight. We flagged down a man on a moped and asked him which road led to Chepp. Instead of answering, he began an incomprehensible rant. We couldn't be sure, but it certainly looked as if he were trying to tell us the road had blown up or washed out, or never been built. I tried again to get help with directions. I pointed my arm down a road to our left and said, "Chepp?" The man nodded firmly and said, "Yes."

    I was satisfied. I don't know what made Nathan uneasy about this exchange, but I'm glad he was. He pointed his arm to the right and looked at the man questioningly, "Chepp?"

The man looked back at Nathan and said, "Yes."

Something critical was being lost in translation.

We smiled politely and thanked the man as he drove off. We waited at the intersection for fifteen minutes before another moped driver passed. He had a few more words in his vocabulary than the first man had, and his directions gave us confidence. We got back onto our bikes to peddle.

For three hours we rode without seeing another human being. We kept a slow but steady pace through the largest protected deciduous forest in Southeast Asia. At the two-hour mark, we came to a very serious washout. It made the road impassable to cars and gave us confidence. We had feared much worse. Instead of having to turn back, we were easily able to walk our bikes through shallow water to the other side. We patted ourselves on the back for having the courage to go on, even when others told us that it was impossible. When the three-hour mark hit, the glory of our courage had worn off, and exhaustion was beginning to set in. We had no idea where we were, or how far we had gone.

In the distance, a man on a moped appeared, riding toward us. When he reached us, he stopped his moped and pointed behind him. We nodded our heads and said, "Chepp," to make it clear that we were heading to where he had just come from. He shook his head at us and said emphatically, "*No*."

We were puzzled. Was this not the route to Chepp? I pointed again and changed the intonation in my voice to make it a question. "Chepp?" The man nodded yes. Then he said, "No."

He used sign language to explain that he hadn't come from Chepp. He had come from Kampong Sra Loa but had to turn around because the road ahead was impassable. We didn't understand how this could be, until we noticed that his entire moped was caked in mud, all the way up to the light on the handlebars. Turning around would have crushed our spirits. I could sense Nathan's trepidation at ignoring such a clear directive not to continue, but we had come too far not to try. I stubbornly mimed to the man that we could carry the bikes over our heads if we had to. He laughed, then sped off.

"We'll be fine. We can't turn around now." I reassured us both. Nathan groaned, cursed under his breath, then got back to peddling.

Over the course of the next two hours, we forged a dozen or more washouts. None of them were so severe that we couldn't roll our bikes next to us as we walked. I was just beginning to mock the warnings we had received as excessively dramatic when it came into sight. It stretched as far as the eye could see, a shiny grey expanse, not of mud as we had suspected, but something much worse. Clay. We rode as far as we could, but when we hit the pit we were immobilized. Our bikes collected and held tight to the globs of heavy clay. It stuck to the wheels, forks, chains, gears and brakes, until the tires could no longer spin. Our bikes went from being twenty pounds each, to being eighty pounds. Our shoes caked-up instantly, making it impossible for us to lift our feet without losing them. The only way through was to carry our packs on our backs, our bikes on our shoulders, and our shoes at our belts. Before we could carry our bikes, we needed to clean them. I couldn't lift mine off the ground or roll it to move it closer to a mud puddle, so Nathan dropped his and came back to help me get closer to the water. We spent the next thirty minutes kneeling in slick clay puddles with our hands alternately dipping into the murky water and digging at our bike parts, to clean them. When they were finally clean enough, and light enough to carry, we untied our things. We cleaned our shoes as best we could, tied them to our belts, and began to portage.

It took about half an hour to go 400 feet. When we had exhausted ourselves completely, we put our bikes down to rest. We were surrounded by clay, fatigued, and we had eaten our last shrimp snack an hour earlier. The sky was growing dark with the threat of rain. Nathan was on edge. It hadn't occurred to me that we were at risk of becoming trapped in the middle of a forty-mile stretch of clay and mud at the start of a torrential downpour, but it *had* occurred to him. He was beginning to panic at the very real possibility that the entire road could turn into to the same mucky hell as where we were standing. If that happened, we wouldn't make it to Chepp by dark, if at all. Spiders and scorpions came out in the dark, which meant that we couldn't afford to rest for long. Our increasingly dire situation helped keep our adrenaline and legs pumping. The pit took us over two hours to trudge through. By the time we had reached the other side, it was mid-afternoon, and we were out of water. We were covered from head to toe in mud and clay, and our sweaty clothes smelled wretched. We had been on the road for seven-and-a-half hours, one of us hungover and the other sleep deprived. There was nothing to do but peddle.

Two hours later, when we finally reached Chepp, we were delirious with thirst. We stopped at the first shop we came to and drank water until our stomachs hurt. We wasted no time in asking for Xuan Youthara. A woman sitting at a fruit shake stand nearby knew him. She made a phone call, and he arrived on a moped five minutes later. He gave us each a disapproving once over, then shook his head at the woman who had called him, as if to blame her for his obligation to take care of us. She started laughing, then shooed him with her hands to encourage him to remove the mud-caked foreigners from her shop. We were a mess. Xuan turned, and waved for us to follow him. He didn't speak English, but by his expression, I could tell he couldn't believe Trong Tri hadn't warned him about what he was getting into.

He brought us to his stilt house and had his wife roll out a bamboo mat for us to sleep on. He had six kids, all of whom were curious about the unannounced guests. His sixteen-year-old daughter followed me to the rain collector to watch me bathe. I couldn't figure out how women bathed without standing naked in front of their entire family. The rain collector was the only water, and it was out in the open for all to see from the balcony of the stilt house. Removing anything more than my shoes and socks seemed inappropriate. I used the small baggie of powdered detergent the girl gave me, to wash my face, hands, and feet. I'm sure she thought I needed some lessons in personal hygiene after watching me, but she smiled pleasantly anyway. Once cleaned up, Nathan and I relaxed for a few hours before dinner.

Xuan's wife fed us, his children laughed with us, and when we offered, they refused to take anything in return for their hospitality.

That night, Nathan slept soundly. He woke refreshed and ready to get on the road. I, on the other hand, didn't sleep a wink. I was exhausted, but eager to hit the road too, to avoid the heat.

As we peddled away that morning, I rolled up next to Nathan. "Did you experience the need to use a toilet in the last eighteen hours?"

Nathan laughed uncomfortably, "No. Why?"

"Well, I...there was some confusion regarding the location of the family bathroom."

"What do you mean confusion? Wasn't there an outhouse somewhere? I just peed in the bushes near the front stairs like Xuan's sons did."

I could feel my ears getting hot beneath my helmet, but went on, "I've always considered my regularity a blessing."

Nathan stopped his bike so suddenly that I had to turn around and come back to him. "What did you do?" He demanded.

"I asked Xuan's daughter where the bathroom was. I used the Khmer word and everything. I knew she understood me. She pointed toward the garden."

"You *pooped* in their garden?!" Nathan was starting to enjoy himself. "Wow. Like, in their vegetables?"

"*No!* I didn't poop in their vegetables. I went near a banana tree. There was no outhouse. It was a garden. I really didn't want to do it, but I didn't have the luxury of time."

Nathan got back on his bike and started peddling fast. He yelled over his shoulder, "I want to be as far away from here as possible when Xuan finds out what you did."

Ditches are for Napping

From Xuan's home in Chepp, we rode to Tbeng Meanchey, a fairly developed town. Several hotels were listed in our guidebook, so we knew we could look forward to a comfortable night's rest. Our primitive map of the road between Chepp and Tbeng Meanchey showed no intersections, but we passed six or seven in the first two hours. Nathan chose our route and we peddled. I had absolute faith in his ability to get us where we were going, but I could tell the decisions were taking a toll on him. As we peddled farther and farther into the jungle, he worried we were covering ground that we would have to turn around and cover again. His mood sank.

After four hours we finally saw the first indication that we were on the right track. It felt as though we had been riding for twice as long as we had. My body was tired, and my brain was cloudy. Had Nathan not been present for the last hour of the ride, I'm positive I would have curled up in a ditch for a nap. The ditches looked so soft and inviting. I had never been so exhausted both physically and mentally in my life. It had been almost forty-eight hours since I had slept. It was painful to be alive. As we rode, I required breaks every fifteen minutes and complained endlessly about my saddle sores. Nathan was patient. He rode slowly, blocking feral dogs from attacking me when they tried. I was weak. When we finally reached town, we booked a room in the first hotel we saw, and I collapsed on the cool tile floor. I hadn't realized how close I had been to passing out until I found myself sprawled on the ground. Nathan untied our things from the bikes, locked them, then came in to tend to his pitiful companion. I managed to get myself clean enough to crawl into bed for a three-hour nap before dinner. While I slept, Nathan enjoyed air conditioning and cartoons on the first television we had seen for a week.

The next morning, we were both somewhat refreshed from a blissful night of sleep. It was day four of our journey across northern Cambodia, and we were blessed with an overcast sky. Things were looking up. We had a bag full of real food for breakfast and lunch, the road was partially paved, and there were only thirty-eight miles to our next destination. Nathan was especially relieved that the clouds shaded us. He wasn't fond of my strategy to combat sun exposure. I had taken to tying clothes over my head and helmet. It did protect me from the sun, but also made me much less credible when called upon for public relations.

About twelve miles into our ride, we spotted a valley swarming with villagers, all planting the community rice fields. I could have sworn that one of the women was waving at us, so I suggested we drop our bikes on the side of the road to join them. Young men and women of all ages circled us when we reached the rice paddy. Nathan was dragged off to a separate field, and we were both put to work. The villagers considered it lucky to have rice planted by a foreigner, so they pulled us from field to field, to share the luck. I wasn't so sure they'd consider themselves lucky when harvest time came around. We were *highly* unskilled laborers.

The rice paddy was a vast area of murky water and mud that raised dirt paths divided into smaller plots. While Nathan toiled at plopping rice seedlings, five at a time, into the mud, a feisty woman in her twenties heckled me. She found my larger than average buttocks endlessly amusing. She gave it multiple exploratory slaps to judge just how enormous it really was. She invited her friends to touch it, then somewhat embarrassed, offered to let me touch hers. When the novelty of my posterior wore off, she began insisting that I leave Nathan with her. He looked over to find her swooning in his direction.

We helped for half an hour but didn't want to disrupt their day for too long. We waved our goodbyes and they shouted their thanks with smiles and waves of their own. By the time we reached our bikes, the villagers were already back to chattering happily as they worked. The encounter revived us. We felt like we were doing exactly what we set out to do. We were getting to know the Khmer people. It didn't seem possible that those happy villagers could have lived through the reign of the Khmer Rouge, but some of them had. Some of them had family members murdered for being doctors, teachers, or government employees. Some of them might even have been captured and tortured, but they were thriving now. They had risen from their past and moved on. They laughed, played, danced, and loved. It was inspiring to spend time with them. We rode for the rest of the morning in good spirits, thinking about the Khmer heart, which we had been told was bigger than any other.

We made it to a village called Srayong by noon and booked a room in the only guesthouse in town. It didn't have electricity, but our room did have a door and a mosquito net. We tried to rent a moped, but no one was willing to part with their transportation. Instead, we were forced to hire a driver who insisted on putting both of us on the back of his bike. It was a tight squeeze. Nathan did me a real favor by taking the middle, so I didn't have to snuggle up to a stranger. We spent the afternoon exploring the temples of Koh Ker with our driver. He doubled as a tour guide, walking us along red dirt paths to his favorite temples. We had the entire complex, including a seven-tiered pyramid, to ourselves. Most of the temple ruins were covered in thick moss, or being overrun by the jungle, but there were a few sculptures of elephants and lions that remained intact. When the storm clouds started closing in, we headed back to town.

Just as we returned to Srayong, it began to rain. We ran around the market looking for a quick dinner and supplies for the next day while the downpour filled puddles and turned the center of town into a slick, muddy mess. After a bowl of rice and some cabbage soup, we took bucket baths and crawled into our bed. We spent the evening in our room, reading about Siem Reap in our guidebook.

The Last Leg

Day five was one of our shortest days, at just over thirty miles. The overnight rain made for a wonderfully messy and fun ride. By the time we reached Beng Meala, we were covered in mud. There were no guesthouses, so we stayed with a family living near the temple entrance. They didn't have a bed for us but did provide a mosquito net, and the privacy of a room to ourselves. Privacy might be an overstatement. We had three little girls under the age of ten come into the room to help us put up our net. They also found a way to open our window from the outside to peek in and giggle at us.

The ruins at Beng Meala had the same floor plan as Angkor Wat, though they were in much worse condition. Due to their distance from tourist hot spots, they were rarely visited and poorly maintained.

Because we arrived on bikes from the middle of nowhere, we managed to avoid the ticket booth set up outside of town. We gave what money we would have paid for a ticket to a woman who was willing to show us where we could crawl and climb, off the beaten track. She was so thrilled with the tip that she hugged and kissed us both. At one point during the tour, we passed a deep pit in the ground. Our guide pointed and said, "Land mine." She picked up her pant leg and showed us her prosthetic. Proof that leaving marked paths could be a deadly mistake. When we finished exploring, we had dinner at a small restaurant, then made our way back to our rented room for the night.

Despite a restless night on a wood slat floor, we were both ready to get going the next morning, our final day. There were forty-eight miles between us and Siem Reap. We rode twenty-five of them before nine in the morning. When we reached Dom Dek, we stopped for coffee and a rest. I popped another handful of pain killers to dull the saddle soreness, but for the most part, we both felt energized.

We felt great until we were about three miles from our destination. The last push was excruciating. We were so close and so tired. In my life, I have never been as sleep deprived or physically worn out as I was the day we reached Siem Reap.

Our first order of business was cheeseburgers.

Our second order of business was finding our belongings. Minh had given us the name of a hotel in town where he would be staying with our bags and passports. We rode our mountain bikes one last time to deliver them. A man saw us approaching the hotel and ran toward us. He claimed that he was the one picking up our bikes. When we asked about our bags and passports, he said they hadn't arrived yet. I was instantly suspicious. I thought it best to lock the bikes before discussing anything with the stranger. Once our bikes were secured, we turned to the man, who was becoming extremely agitated. He asked for the keys to our bike locks so that he could ship them back to Stung Treng, but he didn't know the name Minh. I refused to hand him the keys. Instead, I walked to the front desk to speak with a receptionist. The stranger tried discouraging me from doing this by telling me that the receptionist didn't know anything about the bike deal. I left the key and a note with reception, for Minh, along with the name of where we were staying. On our walk back to our own hotel, Nathan tried to convince me that everything was all right, that Minh wouldn't cheat us. We called Minh as soon as we reached a phone. He cheerfully informed us that he was on his way and would get in later that night. He didn't mention anything about a middleman at the hotel. I am convinced that it was a conman who had heard we would be showing up and wanted to trick us into giving up the bikes.

In the end, it all worked out just fine. Minh showed up at our hotel that night with our things. He stood transfixed as we recounted the obstacles we had faced, and the kindness we had received along the way. When we finished, he admitted, "That was a bigger adventure than I thought it would be. I'm so happy that you enjoyed it, but to be honest, I'm not sure I will tell anyone about this route." He laughed, shook both of our hands, and turned to go. Over his shoulder he called, "I think you have seen more of Cambodia than I have!"

A Real Monkey Business

Once we had our fill of good food, beer, and rest in Siem Reap, we prepared ourselves for a day of temple touring. We rented bicycles with plush seat cushions from a guy hanging around our hotel and headed toward the Angkor Wat Archeological Park. Along the main road leading to the temples was a ticket booth the size of a small airport. I would have thought it *was* an airport if the word *tickets* hadn't been painted in thick black letters on all sides of the building. We approached with caution. We could hear piercing female voices screaming, "Stand here. Stand there. Give me forty dollars."

I gazed upon the scene with wide-eyed disbelief while trying to ignore the ten-year-old girl attempting to pry forty dollars out of my clenched fist.

"Who are these people?" I asked Nathan, as I pointed to the troop of Cambodian adolescents surrounding us. I was worried they could smell our cultural ignorance. Nathan looked just as confused as I felt.

"I have no idea, but I think we're supposed to give this little girl our money." He pointed to the pouting face looking up at us.

"What? She's in fourth grade, tops. Her mom might work here, but her? I don't trust her." I gave the little girl a dangerous look, and she backed up several paces. Her tiny fingers wiggled slowly at her sides, waiting for the next opportunity to strike. The intensity of her glare seemed unnatural for someone so young.

The ticket booth was well constructed. Fifteen parallel rows, each cordoned off and well marked, led to a ticket window. Behind each window sat a flat screen computer monitor and a digital camera. Someone had spent a great deal of money to build the structure, but for some reason, no one wanted to use it. We were encouraged to mill around, spread chaos, and disrupt what order our fellow tourists might bring to the table. A faceless person from behind one of the glass windows thrust a camera on a stick in our direction, snapped a couple of shots, then disappeared. I reluctantly gave my money to the little girl, at which point, she ran away. No one told us to wait for a paper ticket or to move toward the gate. The children we paid did not return. Thankfully, our confusion and curiosity caused us to linger.

About ten minutes later, a different girl, slightly older than the money-grabbers, walked up to us. She eyed us closely, then shuffled through a stack of fifty tickets, each with a photo I.D. on it. It was astonishing. This was a system that raked in hundreds of thousands of dollars a year. As far as I could tell, the government paid fourth graders to take shifts managing foreigners. The whole operation could have been run more efficiently by monkeys. Unfortunately, monkeys hate running ticket booths.

Raining Euphoria

I had assumed that exploring Angkor Wat would be similar to but better than our previous temple visits. I knew it was the largest religious temple on the planet and there were other temples scattered around it. I also knew the entire area was called the Angkor Wat Archeological Park, but that was the limit of my knowledge. We had spoken with countless travelers throughout our journey who'd been to the temples, and who promised that Angkor Wat was as amazing as the guidebooks said it was. In hindsight, I can't be sure whether they were speaking of the Angkor Temple itself or the entire experience.

We left the ticket booth and headed toward Angkor Wat. When we got there, we locked our bikes and entered the temple through its west gate. A sandstone causeway carried us across an impressive moat, swollen with the recent rains. We could see the quincunx of towers at the center of the temple ahead of us. I was strangely underwhelmed. Having explored the jungle ruins of Beng Meala with flashlights and free reign, it was hard to appreciate an Angkor Wat teeming with tourists.

On the other side of the inner gate, the temple opened into a wide expanse of greenery. The grass was healthy and well kept. We stopped to take it in while others rushed past us in a mad dash to the towers. A pasture stretched out for a quarter of a mile, littered with mammoth stone blocks. Some were cracked and covered in the supernatural glow of thick moss; others were unbroken, decorated with the smoothly carved figures of dancing women. The immense ruin fragments looked to have been smashed and scattered by the hands of a giant, bent on destruction. Ancient libraries stood on both sides of the central path. Two Cambodian children ran from one to the other, playing hide-and-seek. They darted playfully around irritated tourists, who were trying unsuccessfully to snap the perfect picture. The little boy and girl were oblivious to their surroundings. They were still too young to be enlisted by desperate parents in the tireless effort of extracting money from tourists. Their responsibility was to keep track of one another, nothing more. I couldn't help but smile at their innocent play. They lived in the shadow of one of the greatest temples known to man, and it was a part of them. The moment was almost ruined by a British man behind me, who grumbled at how inconsiderate it was to let children interfere with the tourist experience. I closed my eyes and imagined turning to him with my worst British accent, "Yes, how right you are. Inconsiderate indeed! Having children! Letting them run around like small adults, without a care in the world! The audacity. Call the Queen, discipline these children. Force them to drink tea."

Nathan looked over at my closed eyes and shook my shoulder. "Everything all right?" I nodded and gave him a mischievous smile.

We climbed the highest tower and enjoyed the view from almost 150 feet above the ground. Hot air balloons were floating in the distance. Surely, they were carrying buckets of grumpy tourists, complaining about the indecency of wind and its disruption of the tourist experience. The contradicting elements of the whole situation didn't work for me. Ruins versus hot air balloons. The scene didn't fill me with wonder, no matter how much the guidebook said it would. I got a dirty look from Nathan when I mentioned that the upper tower smelled like cat urine. Apparently, he was a little less underwhelmed than I was.

By the time we left Angkor Wat, I was starting to feel embarrassed at how empty I felt after having visited it. I thought we had seen the most magnificent thing the Archeological Park had to offer, and I was disappointed. Who goes to Angkor Wat and leaves disappointed? I decided that Nathan should be informed that his travel partner had no appreciation for art or culture. She was a schmuck.

I was quiet as we mounted our rental bicycles and continued toward the rest of the park. I had no idea what to expect for the remainder of our day, but I thought it best to prepare a small speech regarding my lack of appreciation. Perhaps, one that included an apology for the mention of cat urine.

What happened next was something out of a dream. The road narrowed, then turned to dirt. Traffic thinned, then disappeared. We found ourselves riding in silence through a forest that looked hundreds, maybe thousands of years old. Trees jutted from the ground and rose straight into the clouds, their thick trunks damp with mist, the dense musk of healthy earth lingered all around us. I looked back in a panic, almost certain I had been transported through time, hoping Nathan was still with me. His eyes were wide too, taking it all in. He rode up next to me so that we could continue side by side. We came to another moat. A bridge lined with stone warriors, ten times the size of any man, spanned the channel of deep green water. Each chiseled guardian held its arms out, muscles bulging, to support a serpent, which stretched from one end of the bridge to a colossal stone gateway several hundred feet ahead. We walked our bikes respectfully as we passed each set of unwavering gray eyes. The whole scene was surreal; the place was bigger than time itself. The jungle had tried to reclaim these ruins and failed.

When we reached the gate, we realized we were entering Angkor Thom, or in English, Capitol City. Its outer walls stretched as far as we could see into the jungle. The dirt path we had been traveling continued ahead, through a thick stand of trees. We got back on our bikes and peddled slowly, trying to savor every detail. Eventually, the path widened, and the trees opened to reveal the temple of Bayon, at the center of Angkor Thom. Over four dozen towers rose from the ruins. On all four sides, serene faces were carved into gray rock, each with an eerie smile. We were alone in the temple as we wound our way through the tight corridors to examine the Buddhist and Hindu bas-reliefs. We climbed to the highest level to inspect the mysterious faces keeping watch over the city. In the distance, we could see the orange robes of approaching monks as they made their way to the temple for prayer. I started to feel better about my reaction to Angkor Wat. There was no contradiction here. We were walking the halls of a living temple, surrounded by the past, yet grounded in the present. Monks came and went, and local children played in the grass at the forest's edge.

Leaving Bayon, I understood the true wonder of Angkor. Exploring the ruins of great civilizations past has an almost magical ability to wake us up, to tie us to our ancestors with awe and pride. We walked among weathered stone blocks and cracking pillars, bearing witness to their slow battle with the relentless jungle. It gave us a different perspective on the passage of time, how fleeting it was, and how lucky we were to be a part of it.

Other than occasional ticket checks, there was essentially no supervision. Visitors were trusted to explore, climb, and photograph almost everything at their own risk. We found our way to a number of other temples within Angkor Thom's walls, including the Royal Palace and Baphuon, a pyramid structure. We exited the city through the northern gate and continued exploring, first Preah Khan, then Ta Prohm.

As the park was closing, we found ourselves at the farthest corner of its vast network of roads. The air became thick with mist. At first, the rain came softly, tiny droplets rinsing dust from roadside rice paddies, but it quickly transformed into a violent downpour. We rode our bikes through the meanest thunderstorm we had seen in five months. We laughed uncontrollably as we raced on gravel and red-dirt roads with mud flying and our clothes sticking to us. We laughed with relief at having arrived in Siem Reap at all. We laughed with the realization that we had experienced something extraordinary and unexpected in Cambodia. We had fallen in love with the Khmer people, and were connected to Cambodia in a way we hadn't connected to other places. The people were our people. The temples were our temples. Lush rice fields grew our food, and the rain washed the dirt from our skin. We were Cambodians. That final bike ride was joyful and heartbreaking. Our experience in Cambodia was coming to a close.

Before the week was out, we were on a bus back to Bangkok.

Chapter Five

Thailand (Again)
Eeny, Meeny, Miny, Moe, Catch a Tiger by the…

Bangkok was a different experience the second time around. We were practically residents of the Kingdom. I half expected locals to speak Thai around me; my integration was nearly complete. We knew where to eat, what to eat, where to stay, and how much to pay. Our numbers were a little rusty, but they came back quickly. We spent almost a week in the city, doing the things we had been too nervous to do the first time around. We took in movies at the theater downtown and stayed out late visiting bars with live music. We gave advice to other travelers and shared our stories. I felt grown up, experienced, and knowledgeable.

We could have flown from Cambodia to Malaysia, which was our next destination, but there was one more thing I wanted to do in Thailand. I wanted to go to The Tiger Monastery. When we tired of sharing our sage advice with mildly interested strangers in Bangkok, we booked a day trip to Kanchanaburi, home of the Tiger Monastery. It was not a cheap excursion. Nathan agreed to go with me in return for a future favor, even though I suspected he wanted to go as much as I did.

When we arrived at the gate in the late afternoon, we wasted no time buying our tickets. Once inside the monastery, we walked to a dusty canyon about a quarter of a mile from the entrance. It was surrounded on three sides by sheer rocks that rose forty feet from a sandy patch of dirt where the tigers were tethered. There were nearly thirty tigers, lounging lazily beneath shade umbrellas, sunning themselves on flat rocks, and rolling in the sand.

There is some controversy regarding places like these. Are the tigers drugged? Are they well fed? Where does the money go when we hand it over at the ticket booth?

All I can say for sure is that the tigers did not look like they were being mistreated. They were well fed, and they were loved. The monks and volunteers who cared for them were passionate about their work. Many of them were willing to talk to anyone who would listen about the dwindling numbers of these majestic creatures.

If you thought that monkeys were dangerous, which I hope you did, then it should be obvious that tigers belong in an entirely different and terrifying category of dangerous. The largest of these cats could have crushed my Toyota Tercel with a front paw; therefore, I was appreciative of all measures taken to maintain a safe environment for visitors.

Tourists lined up and were given a list of rules: no fast movements, loud noises, rough-housing, bright colors, purses or scarves, and no wandering around without a monk or a volunteer holding your hand to guide you. Our cameras were taken, and we were allowed to enter the cavern several at a time. A monastery volunteer took pictures using each of our cameras, while we sat with, stood next to, or attempted to pet one of the lounging creatures.

The man behind me began to argue with a volunteer. He wished to carry his own camera into the cavern and have the freedom to take pictures of whatever he wanted. He was certain that the volunteer with his camera wasn't going to be talented enough to get clear shots. The volunteer had more patience than I would have had. She gently explained that he would be in danger if he started darting around with a flashing camera in front of a six-hundred-pound cat. He finally agreed.

As I was led away with my guide, I conspiratorially whispered to the woman he had been harassing that she should've let him learn the hard way.

I never imagined being so close to an animal so capable of eating my head in a single bite. The lions in the creepy Cambodian petting zoo had been frightening, but in a fight between lions and tigers, there is no doubt in my mind that the tigers would win. Their muscles rippled under shining coats, square heads moved slowly from visitor to visitor, taking careful stock of their surroundings. Their steady gazes demanded respect. I am almost certain that even though the tigers were chained, the people were the submissive creatures in that canyon. Nathan and I had our pictures taken with several tigers, and then we wandered around the monastery meeting monks and watching baby tigers play.

On our way back to Bangkok, I took a look at the pictures that the volunteers had snapped of our visit. I was tickled to discover a photo of Nathan and the largest tiger. In it, Nathan appears to be grabbing the creature by its testicles. The expression on Nathan's face is strangely defiant. One eyebrow is lifted, and his mouth is curled in a wicked smirk. The tiger seems indifferent, laying on its back, hind legs splayed out to either side of his visitor. When confronted, Nathan claimed that he was not grabbing any part of the tiger. He claimed that he was merely petting the only available spot on the relaxing animal. His claims were, and still are, difficult to believe.

Having visited the tigers, it was time to move on. We were ready to continue our journey south, to Malaysia. The night before our departure from Thailand, Nathan found me sitting on my ankles in front of the toilet, moaning in disbelief. He didn't have to ask what was wrong. My silver ring glimmered beneath five inches of yellowish liquid. He closed the door with a, "I'll just leave you to it then."

It could have been worse. It could have been a portable toilet. I won't carry anything I'm not willing to lose *forever* into one of those things. Later, as we were discussing the incident, Nathan admitted that he had dropped something into a toilet recently too. He said, "I can't remember exactly what it was. Maybe nail clippers, maybe the dental floss."

I had no words. I hoped desperately that the dental floss bit was a joke. There was only one roll of dental floss between the two of us, and it wasn't Nathan's. I had used it earlier that morning.

I stood, staring blankly ahead, momentarily paralyzed by the horror of having flossed with a contaminated dental product. The ever so slight rise in my anxiety level began an anxiety chain reaction. That's how it works with me. Usually, I keep all the things bringing me anxiety tucked away in the cobwebby recesses of my brain. It's the place I kept the nagging feeling that I had an alien twin sister as a child, and then later, as an adult working in retail, the place I kept the vague awareness that my job was slowly murdering me. Before I had time to stop it, my brain had produced a number of items on my most-anxiety-causing list, and I was spewing them out at Nathan.

"What if we have parasites? Do you think we'll have enough money to buy our plane tickets home? Where am I going to live when I get back to the U.S.? Should I be preparing a resume? Are we going to live together? Are we going to be a couple?"

Nathan sat staring at me for several moments, then whispered cautiously, "What just happened?"

I burst out laughing, "Yeah. Sorry. I felt anxious for a second there. You just got a sneak peek into the list of things driving me crazy."

Nathan looked a little relieved, then apologized. "I realize it's getting closer to the end of our trip. I should probably start thinking about what I want to happen when we get back."

I was surprised that he thought so, considering we still had several weeks before returning home. It wasn't like him to be so timely. I wondered if I was rubbing off. I thought it might seem a little self-serving to encourage him to start making some decisions, so I just smiled noncommittally.

Nathan offered to spend the next morning thinking about the future. He wanted some time alone to process, so I selflessly suggested that I spend the morning shopping, to give him the time he needed. When I returned to the hotel room after perusing gift shops, I found him huddled in the fetal position on the bed. He sat up and whimpered, "I have some bad news."

Not what I had been hoping for.

I hesitantly asked, "What bad news?"

Then, he said something unexpected. "I think I have lupus."

"What are you talking about?! I thought you were breaking up with me. Why would you tell me you had bad news? What the hell is wrong with you?"

"Lupus *is* bad news! Don't be ridiculous, I'm not breaking up with you. After I did my thinking, I had some extra time, so I spent it on WebMD and I'm sure, with all of my current symptoms, I have lupus."

I shot back, "You do *not* have lupus. You have the flu. Pull yourself together. You're cut off from the Internet until you're better. Sick people shouldn't be allowed access to WebMD."

That night, despite having lupus, Nathan boarded an overnight train with me, bound for Butterworth, Malaysia. We said goodbye to Thailand for the last time.

Chapter Six

Malaysia
The Melting Pot

The train ride to Butterworth took twenty-three hours. Most of it was spent curled in our sleeper bunks, listening to audio books and eating the Thai candies a lovely Thai woman in the bunk below us gave to us. We got off the train at the Malaysian border to get our passports stamped and our fingerprints taken, then boarded the train for another four hours to our destination. Ten minutes from our stop we both started to feel a little anxious. We realized we had done absolutely no preparation. I know this sounds impossible, to be surprised by the fact that we were unprepared, but that's what happened. We knew there was an island off the coast of Butterworth with UNESCO status, but didn't know the island's name, how we were going to get there, or whether we had to find a boat or a bus to a boat, and we didn't have a map.

Nathan urged me to make some friends. So, I introduced myself to an older couple who turned out to be ex-teachers from the University of Maine, my alma mater. The woman had taught social work while I was there studying biochemistry. We chitchatted while Nathan took a quick look at their guidebook.

Thankfully, Butterworth was a city with sense; the train station, bus terminal, and ferry were all in the same place. From the train station, we walked to the port and took a quick ferry ride to Penang Island, which we had just learned was home to the city of Georgetown, a World Heritage Site known for its culinary delights. Incidentally, the existence of Georgetown, and the term *culinary delights* were the only two things that Nathan had time to learn before the Mainers asked for their guidebook back.

We found a guesthouse several blocks from the ferry terminal with clean rooms and an attached internet cafe. After a couple of hours in our air-conditioned room, we decided to get something to eat. I did a little research on the Internet and learned about Nyonya, a cuisine with both Malay and Chinese flavors. It sounded delicious, so we walked to a traditional Nyonya restaurant for dinner. Nathan ordered a dish called Ayam Buah Keluak. It turned out to be a chicken dish, cooked with the nut of the mangrove tree. I ordered something called Jiew Hu Char, shredded vegetables fried with thinly sliced, dried cuttlefish. The only item that neither of us could stomach was called Cincalok. It was a dipping sauce made out of fermented shrimp. It tasted exactly like fermented shrimp.

On the walk back to our hotel, we started to notice the differences between Malaysia and all the other places we had visited. In Thailand, the streets were crowded with Thai people. In Laos, the rivers were crowded with Laotians. In Vietnam, we saw mostly Vietnamese people, and in Cambodia, there were Cambodians. In Malaysia, there were three distinct populations. There were Indians, Chinese, and Malay people. Each population had its own parts of town, restaurants, shops, and grocery stores.

In addition to the mélange of culture influences, there was another significant difference between Malaysia and the rest of Southeast Asia. In all the other countries, the predominant religion is Buddhism. In Malaysia, just over sixty percent of the population is Muslim.

For me, the appearance of burqas, prayer rooms, and mosques was a familiar and comforting sight. During my time in West Africa, I stayed with a Muslim family and spent all of my time working and living with men and women of the Islamic faith. For Nathan, the experience was new. He had never lived in a place where people's religious beliefs were so much a part of their everyday life.

Betel Nut

Our first full day on Penang began innocently enough. Nathan and I took a guided tour through a spice plantation north of Georgetown. While walking through gardens of ginger, clove, lemongrass, and nutmeg, our guide told us of the betel nut. In India, it is apparently very popular. People chew it in combination with other spices such as clove, tobacco, and cinnamon. We made a mental note to investigate further, when time allowed.

After our tour, we sat down for a drink at the plantation's bar and struck up a conversation with a wise old man. He sternly warned us about one more thing on the monkey most-hated list. I was pleasantly surprised to speak with someone trying, like me, to spread monkey awareness. The man explained soberly how foolish it is to smile at a monkey. "Showing your teeth to a monkey is considered by most monkeys to be a challenge. If you're looking for a fight, you'll have one."

Backpack Like You Mean It

1.5 seconds before someone gets their face ripped off.

He claimed to have seen this exceedingly dangerous misunderstanding firsthand. I think the seriousness with which I received his warning made him think that I was toying with him. Even when I assured him that I knew very well that monkeys can rip people's faces off in the blink of an eye, he looked to Nathan to make sure I wasn't being a smart ass. Nathan shook his head and confirmed, "You're preaching to the choir. She's dead serious. She's been warning me about monkey violence for five months."

When the old man looked back over at me, he smiled jovially and ordered me a margarita. I told Nathan that if he took monkeys more seriously, maybe he would be making friends with wise old men too.

When I finished my margarita, we said our farewells, and spent the rest of the afternoon exploring on our moped. For the most part, the narrow road clung to the coastline. On occasion, the ocean would disappear from view and the road would dip inland for several miles, taking us through lush tropical fruit plantations and dense clusters of durian trees. We ended our tour in Georgetown's Little India. Searching for the betel nut seemed as good an excuse as any to enjoy some Indian food and a lively marketplace.

We parked the bike and went in search of a shop selling, *betel nut for chewing*, per our guide's instructions. The streets of Little India were bustling with activity. Sitar music blasted from every shop, creating a tangle of rhythmless music. Shop owners moved their wares further into the street to encourage business. As the sun went down, the street came alive. The vibrant colors of silk saris, dupattas, and veils spread like a wrinkled rainbow as light caught each, sending a shimmering glow through the gems, beads, and sequins that adorned them. The effect was strangely reminiscent of the colors in a gasoline spill, glistening on black pavement. Bracelets, necklaces, gold jewelry, and precious stones of every shape and size were glimmering in the fluid light.

Headlights, streetlights, shop lights, and the occasional candle lit the darkness. Incense burned on every table and in every storefront. The cloud of sweet smoke rolled thick and low, tightening our chests and stinging our eyes. There were people everywhere. Most were part of the community; they either lived or worked within the limits of Little India. Shop owners wandered from their shops to gossip. Women gathered ingredients for the evening meal. Men advertised their restaurants with loud shouts that could be heard above the music. English-speaking youth offered their services as guides to travelers like us. There was movement everywhere, all at once. The sensory assault was exhilarating.

We strolled through the market, popping our heads into shop after shop, until eventually we stumbled into a tiny stall where a woman sat preparing betel nuts for chewing. She pulled two green leaves from a stack, rubbed them with limestone paste, then pulled out a tray with tiny cups of mysterious ingredients. She expertly tossed a pinch of this and a pinch of that onto the leaves and then pinned the piles together using a whole clove. Proud of our ability to procure this authentic piece of local culture, we decided to celebrate with some delicious Indian cuisine.

After dinner, we returned the rental moped before heading back to our hotel to experiment with our loot. I hate to ruin the surprise for future thrill seekers but chewing these little packets of betel nut cocktail was like eating urinal cakes dipped in shampoo. Our drooling was uncontrollable. Something caused our saliva, teeth, and tongues to turn bright red. It took less than two minutes to change us into pale, drooling, nauseated wretches. Neither of us had any desire to see the betel nut experiment to its end. We spit vigorously but couldn't get rid of the taste or the dizziness. The misery was just beginning. We both curled into the fetal position, Nathan on the bed and me on the floor, each moaning in discomfort while red drool leaked from the corners of our mouths. I can't say for sure how long it lasted. It felt like hours. I was granted the slightest bit of relief when I began violently throwing up my spicy dinner. The relief was a double-edged sword. I felt better but couldn't bring myself to eat Indian food for the remainder of our trip.

When Monkeys Attack

After spending several days on and around Penang, we traveled south to Kuala Lumpur. Arriving in the city, I was surprised to discover that it looked like every big city in the United States. For some reason, I had the impression that large cities in other countries wouldn't feel like American cities. They couldn't be as sprawling, as modern, or as clean. I was wrong. Kuala Lumpur is more modern than most U.S. cities, and much cleaner. Its subways and light rail stations weaved their way between twenty-story shopping centers, grocery stores, and university districts. There were cars, trucks, motorcycles, buses, and trains zooming in every direction. Although there were many differences, there was something familiar and natural about exploring the city. Getting around was easy, and the people were friendly and helpful. I knew immediately that I wanted to spend a significant amount of time in Kuala Lumpur to begin our re-acclimation into a more Western lifestyle, and to enjoy some of its luxuries.

Shortly after our arrival in Kuala Lumpur, I was forced to come to terms with my heretofore unmentioned illness. Chronic head swelling. Over the course of the previous three months, I had begun to notice, and truly suffer from, a rare condition. My head changed size, rather drastically, while I slept. I was certain that Nathan agreed with me on some level because he regularly confirmed my head size on a scale of one to ten, with accuracy, when asked. Accuracy was a function of how closely his head size rating matched my own, objective rating. At first, he didn't like this exercise, I could tell. He worried I was laying an intricate woman trap for him, manipulating him somehow, for reasons unknown to him. When he realized I wasn't, he began to enjoy the process of evaluating my head size every morning. Most of the time, I could live a normal life. However, there were some situations when this very real illness brought pain and self-loathing.

One such occasion was our visit to the Batu Caves. We enjoyed a fantastic tour through the winding chambers, viewing species of insect never before seen in any other location. Our guide was a quirky young woman with social anxiety, who eventually warmed up to our jokes. The only downside to cave exploring was walking in front of Nathan. He pointed his flashlight at the back of my skull, projecting my oversized head shadow onto stalactites and cavern walls. A gasp left his mouth every time he caught a glimpse of my giant head shadow.

After the fifth or sixth gasp, I hissed over my shoulder, "Nathan! Will you please quit doing that!"

He acted apologetic, "Oh, sorry. The size of your head just catches me by surprise every so often. It's an involuntary reaction."

While enduring Nathan's ridicule, I had to remain ever vigilant. The Batu Caves were crawling with monkeys. I saw my first monkey attack. I was disappointed that the incident had almost no effect on Nathan. I had always assumed that his respect and fear of monkeys would kick in when he saw a ferocious primate leap into the air with teeth and claws wildly tearing at the ignoramus trying to get a closer look, but I was wrong. He was unflappable, almost disinterested. I, on the other hand, became paralyzed with fear. I made Nathan clear the path ahead of me and tried to keep my breathing calm. Monkeys hate cowards.

Despite the odds, we made it back to Kuala Lumpur unscathed. On our second full day in the city, Nathan decided to cash-in on his favor for having accompanied me to the Tiger Monastery. He requested that we spend a day exploring the largest, walk-in, open-air aviary in the world. I dislike birds, but I accepted his choice of activity with a pleasant smile and a promise that I would genuinely look for a bird for which I felt fondness. I spent most of the day taking as many pictures of Nathan and birds as I could, in hopes that he would settle for excellent pictures in place of visiting another aviary at *any* point in the future.

When it was time to get out of the big city, we headed east to explore Tioman Island off the coast of Mersing. I was in charge of planning our journey. It was the first time that Nathan sat back and let me make all of the decisions for both of us. It was also the last time.

Bad Information

Six months earlier, while I toiled over hostel bookings and worried about travel routes and timelines, I would never have believed it possible that a moment would come when I, the anal-retentive planner, would make Nathan, the disorderly free wheeler, uncomfortable with my total lack of planning. Nathan is a man who I would describe not so much as an adventure seeker, but as an adventure magnet. He doesn't go looking for trouble, but he also doesn't anticipate the potential for it. From time to time, he finds himself in situations which, with a little planning, could have been avoided. He has a Houdini complex, as far as I can tell; a strange attraction to situations where he has to wiggle his way from a tight spot. He once explained his methodology thus: planning is an adventure-potential killer. The more you plan, the less likely you are to stumble into something wonderful, learn something unexpected, or be pushed to practice flexibility.

At the time of his explanation, I probably scoffed at him, assuming it was an inventive excuse to justify missing plane flights, disregarding schedules, and having to make preparations of any kind.

I'll admit now that there is something to Nathan's theory. Too much planning can take the spontaneity and even the fun potential from almost anything. It takes time and practice to find the thin line between too much and not enough preparation. When Nathan realized I was searching for that line, it was already too late for him to intervene.

Nathan falsely assumed that I did my research before waking him at seven fifteen for a nine o'clock bus to Mersing, a city on the eastern shore of Malaysia. He accepted my timeline willingly, without asking any questions. We got to the bus station, purchased the last two available tickets, and hit the road.

When we arrived in Mersing six hours later, we shuffled across the street to a shop selling ferry tickets to Tioman Island. The existence of this island and its name were the outer limits of the research I had done. We bought tickets from a woman who then asked where we wanted to be dropped off on the island. I replied that it didn't matter because we could always rent a moped. Her eyes shot up to meet mine; then she rolled them.

"I see you have come here with bad information," she mocked. "There are no roads on Tioman."

I think I caught her a bit off guard when I replied, "No. We came here with *no* information, not *bad* information."

I peeked at the map she held and pointed at the northern tip of the island where it said Salang Beach. I told her that's where we wanted to go. We got in line at the ferry terminal with the rest of the mob and were quickly herded onto a boat. Someone asked me where we were going, and I replied confidently, "Salang," a word that Nathan claimed he was hearing for the first time. The crew told us to collect our bags and get off the boat. This confused us. Nathan was certain I had just made our destination up, so he started to argue with the ferry employee.

"Where is this boat going? We'll go there."

The man replied, "Sir, where are *you* going?" They exchanged these exact words back and forth about three times before the man gave up and walked away.

Behind Nathan, a know-it-all tourist decided we needed a translator. He tapped Nathan's shoulder and said, "I think you're on the wrong boat, man."

Nathan replied testily, "How can I be on the wrong boat when I don't even know where my destination is?"

"Your girlfriend said Salang."

"She was just making up words!"

Finally, Nathan looked over at me, flustered. I explained that Salang was a beach on the northern tip of the island. It was too late to change anyone's mind. We were forced to disembark and were sent to timeout for being poor planners, I suspect. We sat on the pier, segregated from all the other passengers who had not gotten on the wrong, unmarked boat. When the second ferry showed up, we were kicked to the back of the line.

A man in a uniform asked Nathan where we were going. Nathan turned to me and shouted across aisles, "Hey Jenny, what was that word you used to get us kicked off the last ferry?"

"Salang."

"Right. We're going to Salang," he said to the crew member. The man nodded. Things were looking up.

It took almost three hours. Just before reaching Salang, all the other tourists on the boat got off. We were tempted to follow, thinking they might all know something that we didn't, but instead we decided to stick it out and wait for Salang. After all, it was the reason we had endured a forty-five-minute timeout.

We had no idea whether accommodations existed, or how much they would cost. Nathan was quietly visualizing his Robinson Crusoe survival techniques as we pulled up to a dock. Something seemed funny to the crew as we waved our goodbyes and trudged onto shore. It all became clear when we checked in to the only hotel complex for miles. Walking along the dock toward the reception area, Nathan said, "There's no way this is Salang Beach. We're not at the tip of the island."

I was skeptical that the crew of the boat would have the audacity. "No way. They wouldn't have dropped us off somewhere else."

When we got to the reception counter, Nathan casually asked the receptionist, "So, how far to Salang beach?"

"Twenty minutes by boat," the man replied distractedly, as he checked us in. Nathan looked over at me. I stared straight ahead, not wanting to give him the satisfaction. Then I noticed the picture of Salang beach, a place that we were obviously *not*, sitting on the counter in front of us. I conceded. "OK, you're right. *That* is Salang Beach. We've been had."

In hindsight, the crew's laughter made total sense. They thought themselves clever for ditching their last two uniformed passengers at the nearest dock, so they could get home faster. It turned out just fine. Our hotel had delicious food, and a vacant hillside bungalow waiting for us. We stayed for almost a week. I was forgiven for my poor research skills but informed I would no longer have complete control.

Tioman is the tropical island that everyone wishes they could be stranded on. It has mountains cloaked in uncharted jungles, white sand beaches, and surprisingly few people to disrupt its charm.

Apart from a few lizard run-ins, our time on Tioman was peaceful and productive. We read books, wrote in our journals, and slept well. One blazing hot afternoon, as we sat in the shade, dangling our feet from the side of our bungalow's porch, Nathan admitted that it was finally time for him to make a plan. I was ecstatic. I had waited almost six months to make my own plans for the next one to ninety years with Nathan. I was looking forward to having something to look forward to.

If I didn't know better, I would say that Nathan had spent six months trying to convert me to the dark side. The side where no one makes plans, and no one ever gets what they expect, and people don't look at watches. Our entire trip, he had refused to map out more than a few days, not wanting to inadvertently eliminate any opportunities for adventure. I'll admit, I had adopted some of his tactics. I was less worried about always knowing where we were going, and more willing to make quick, uninformed decisions for the fun of it.

I sat patiently waiting, as Nathan nodded his head, deep in thought. He finally said, "Let's move somewhere together." And that was that.

I considered the matter of our future settled. For Nathan, it had just been plucked from the sweet depths of oblivion and placed center stage, for him to worry about. Where would he work? Where would we live? Would we be thrown into an economy prepared to eat us alive, spit us out, and trample us below the poverty line? None of this mattered to me. I couldn't do much about it until we flew home, so I didn't let it get me down. Instead, I took a page from Nathan's book, and decided to live in the moment. Thankfully, I like knowing how much money I have in the moment, so I counted our combined ringgit. Our cash reserves had dipped low enough to leave us with mere pennies after the purchase of our return ticket to Mersing, so we organized seats on the next ferry back to the mainland.

Chapter Seven

Singapore
It's Only Money

From Mersing, we decided to make our next stop Singapore. Buses heading for the border were incredibly cheap, and one left every fifteen minutes. The ride took just under five hours. We were dropped off in downtown Singapore just after six in the evening. I admit, our tourism had gotten terribly sloppy. When we should have been making plans and locating maps in our down time, we had taken to doing just about anything else. As a result, we stumbled into Singapore's late afternoon sun with no idea where we were, where we would be sleeping, or how we would get there. A group of three French girls passed, looking down intently at a map. I asked to take a peek, and wouldn't you know it, they had an extra they were willing to part with, and we happened to be a ten-minute walk from backpacker row.

We took our time walking to a hostel. The one we had decided on was in Singapore's version of Little India, so we let our senses guide us on a minitour before finding a place to drop our things. The brightly colored garments, elaborate desserts, and the scent of burning incense were familiar, yet slightly more sophisticated. Shops were more elaborately decorated, and their patrons more finely dressed than we had seen in Georgetown's Little India. Along the busy street, there were dozens of shops carefully displaying a greater variety of fresh vegetables and fruits than we had ever seen. There was an abundance of everything. It was a more tightly controlled yet equally authentic Little India. Crowds of people hustled from one place to another, shopping, visiting, living their lives.

We found the hostel we had picked out from the map and discovered it was full. We walked from hostel to hostel and found each one at capacity. It was getting dark when we finally stumbled into a hostel with the last two beds in Little India. For the first time on our entire trip, we stayed in a dorm. A tiny bunk bed, in a room with nine others, cost us each thirty dollars. Singapore was *not* cheap. The price of one night in Singapore was the same as ten nights in almost any hotel in Thailand.

While Nathan slept, I spent the early mornings writing letters to the other people in our dorm room.

Dear Lady who coughs up what I can only assume are apricot-sized balls of mucus every twenty minutes and loudly swallows them,

What is your condition? Is it communicable? Was it a dream, or did you really put your feet on my head last night?
Also, you snore.

Kindly,
The woman in bunk 4

Dear Lady who brushes her teeth and tongue so vigorously at five thirty in the morning that she starts to throw up,

Did you have an unusually animated conversation with yourself in the bathroom just now?
Did I hear you kissing the mirror?
Also, what could you possibly have packed so deeply in your bag and so tightly wrapped in plastic that it took you fifteen minutes of rustling to get it out in the middle of the night?

Kindly,
The woman in bunk 4

Dear man who stole my towel after I used it,

I saw you collecting the towels of every woman staying in this room. I know you don't work here. What is your game? Also, I don't think anyone else noticed, but I saw you sniffing your bunk mate's dirty laundry. Don't come near me.

Kindly,
The woman in bunk 4

Most of our time in Singapore was spent exploring on foot. Kuala Lumpur had impressed me with its modern architecture, timely transportation, and cleanliness, but Singapore was its superior in almost every way.

Singapore is a city from the future. Its buildings are gravity defying. Its bridges are masterpieces, and its artistic approach to efficiency is inspiring. We walked through a cluster of restaurants on the water, all canopied by the same metallic wings of a giant protective sculpture. Each building was painted in the same style, though glowing a different color. They were uniform yet pleasantly unique. The canopy structure snaked from every corner to a central courtyard, common to each restaurant, yet owned by none. Fountains dotted the cement tiles, some gushed icy water that lingered just long enough to chill the patrons' toes, others jumped high into the air from one spot to another as people did their best to stay clear.

We crossed a bridge whose walkway was encompassed by the twisting arms of a double helix. In the distance, three towers, each almost sixty stories, dominated the skyline. They were the legs of an exclusive hotel climbing hundreds of feet to support a massive boat, hovering above us. In every direction, there seemed to be an architectural marvel jutting from the depths of the city.

We found our way to the financial district when we tired of exploring museums and shopping centers. There's nothing like walking through the financial district of one of the most successful and driven economies on the planet to sow the seeds of panic for one's own financial stability. It was necessary to visit the Fountain of Wealth after facing thousands of men and women wearing suits worth more than my savings account. We heard that if we walked three times around the fountain with our hands in the water, while making a wish, it would come true. I silently did a wealth wish for the two of us. It was the largest fountain in the world, which I hoped made it the best conduit for wishes.

That evening we sat in a country western pub, planning our trip to the zoo. For those of you wondering what a country western pub in Singapore looks like, it looks like a normal pub, with three or four cowboy hats hanging from the walls. The Singapore zoo was our last stop before heading back to Malaysia the next evening. We spent our second night in the same room filled with different strangers.

Dear husband and wife in the twin bed creaking above mine,

I would really, really appreciate it if you didn't do what you are doing. I am worried about the bed frame buckling, which would likely result in my death.
Also, it's gross.
Also, the guy in bunk six is watching you intently.

Kindly,
The woman in bunk 4

The next day, I woke Nathan when I finished writing my letters to bunk mates. We made it to the zoo several minutes before it opened, which was well worth it, because the facility was incredible. Who knew there were so many species of monkey? With careful observation, I discovered several more things that monkeys hate. Some were surprising, others not. For instance, some species of monkeys hate children. We stumbled into a performance for elementary-aged kids about the importance of protecting the environment. During the show, a monkey swung its way to a rope hanging above a group of little girls and began to urinate on their heads. I can't be certain whether it was the children, or the fact that they were talking during a presentation. It was probably both.

Also, monkeys hate fake rocks, being locked up, mustard, their own feces, and unattractive women.

We spent a full day viewing animals, then found a bus to Melaka. We might have stayed one more night in Singapore if we had been able to find a place to sleep, but even our meager dorm beds had been booked by other guests. Lack of accommodation was one of two reasons our time in Singapore was so brief; the other was our dwindling bank account balances.

Chapter Eight

Malaysia (Again)
Birthday Wish

We arrived in Melaka with enough time to find a guesthouse before dark. I had been hesitant about going to another town whose claim to fame was old buildings, but Nathan assured me that it was on every guidebook's top ten list. I suspected that he wanted to spend my birthday in a World Heritage site to make me feel young in comparison. It wasn't much of a comfort—being young compared to a cobblestone road, but I was thrilled once we'd had a chance to explore. Melaka was the quaintest river town I had ever visited. A lazily flowing canal wandered through the center of the old city. On both banks, an elegantly decorated walkway weaved through small shops, restaurants, and shaded parks. In the evenings, the soft glow of streetlamps and decorative lights dropped shimmering reflections onto the water's surface.

When I woke up on the morning of my thirtieth birthday, our first full day in Melaka, did I expect to have a teenage Malaysian boy on his knees, serenading me with a sweet little ditty called "Bad Love" by My Chemical Romance?

No.

Did a birthday miracle make this happen?

Yes.

Nathan suggested visiting the torture museum for my birthday. It was tempting, but I wanted to spend the day exploring the Melakan History, and Weird-Life-Sized-Creepy-Mannequin Museum instead. The museum itself was a bit of a disappointment, but on our way out the door, a group of eight teens came running up to us. They begged us to buy some pickled fruits. It was not the first time we had seen these snacks. We knew firsthand that pickled fruits were atrocious. They combine the worst of pickle flavor with unripe, bad fruit. I had been lured in by their vibrant colors and asymmetrical shapes the first time I had seen them. They were hard to miss, and a fixture in most marketplaces in Malaysia.

I threw my hands into the air to silence their frenzied pleas. I asked calmly, but forcefully, "Who are you all working for? And, why do you to want us to buy these terrible snacks so badly?" This silenced them for a moment, then a mousy girl in the back whispered, "Please buy them."

The group started giggling uncontrollably. I got the strange feeling that they wanted to get rid of them, but not because they needed the money.

I tried again to get some useful information, "Listen, I'm going to be honest. We *hate* these." I pointed to the plastic jug of brightly colored fruit and pretended to gag. "But, I'm also curious. Why are you so intent on selling them? What's going on?"

We learned that the kids were in a citywide competition, to complete a list of tasks while running around looking for clues and asking for help from strangers. Nathan thinks the task in question might have been to sell something to a tourist for a 500 percent markup, because they were asking for three dollars.

While explaining their situation, the kids made a serious mistake. They showed desperation, and when negotiating, that is a very dangerous thing to do. Nathan thinks I may have gone too far, but kids these days need to learn proper negotiating strategy. Never show how motivated you are to buy or sell. I did the group a service. First, I negotiated down the price to two dollars. Then, I requested that one of the boys get down on one knee to serenade me. This would have been much less humiliating if it hadn't been in a public market. People stopped to take photos, all curious to know what was happening. When I felt this young man had earned his two dollars, (it certainly wasn't the pickled snacks for which we were negotiating), I shook his hand and told him the money was well earned. Nathan paid him more than our agreed price out of pity. Everyone was thrilled, and the boy was giddy to have completed his team's task in such an unexpected way.

On our last day in Melaka, we visited the Maritime Museum, which I thought would have been more appropriately named, The Portuguese and Outer-Space Museum. There were two things about it that baffled me. The first was a giant statue of an American astronaut. The second, was the fact that the museum was built in the hull of a fifteenth-century Portuguese trading ship, but the inside was designed like the Starship Enterprise. I considered finding an employee to question but decided that some things are better left a mystery.

Goodbye Worms, Hello America

From Melaka, we made our way back to Kuala Lumpur, to spend the final few days of our six-month adventure. We were listless, hanging in a strange limbo between travel and home, unable to do much more than eat, sleep, and organize our bags. The most exciting activity we could manage was eating custard. Nathan found a vendor in the basement of a deserted building and insisted we visit every day. Watching the hours pass was excruciating. I felt guilty that we weren't doing and seeing more with the time we had left in Malaysia, but we couldn't help it. Our anticipation was paralyzing. I couldn't wait to see my family and friends, and to begin the process of settling into a routine again.

Our last act as travelers the morning before our flight, was a de-worming. It wasn't glamorous but it was very necessary. We had been feeling a bit run down since the bike trip in Cambodia. During that trip, we had both suffered from mysterious rashes, fevers, and stomach ailments, which in all likelihood, meant parasitic infection. Medicine was much cheaper in Malaysia than at home, so we figured it might be prudent to expel our unwanted guests.

We picked up two adult doses of de-wormer at the local pharmacy and sat down in a small park to take our medicine. Nathan handed me a chewable chocolate anti-parasitic, then watched, stone faced, as I ate it. When I had finished, he read aloud from the back of the package, "May cause vomiting." That's when I noticed that he hadn't taken his. I had to laugh.

Nathan.

What a gentleman.

Afterword

We made it safely back to the United States. I had myself checked out immediately to ensure my parasitic freeloaders didn't do the same, but Nathan wasn't in a rush to be tested. When pushed, he explained that some people pay handsomely for parasites, to keep themselves thin. He didn't want to throw away a perfectly good revenue stream while we were both experiencing cash flow problems. So far, we haven't had to cash in his worms for food or lodging.

We fell right back into our American lives. We got cell phones, cars, and jobs. We worried about things like buying a mattress, Internet access, and electricity bills. We got used to using a trashcan instead of throwing our garbage out of our windows.

One morning, about two months after our return, Nathan made bacon for breakfast and offered a couple of pieces to me. I wrinkled my nose, "Ew. Thanks, but I can't eat the stuff that isn't crispy. Chewing fat is weird."

He nodded absentmindedly, as if to say he understood, then froze. His eyes incredulously met mine, "Wait. You can't eat chewy bacon, but you can eat a tarantula?"

He had a point. What had happened to me? I made a promise to continue pursuing adventurous endeavors, no matter where we were. Nathan pledged his full support. When a week later, he got home from work to discover I had procured two pregnant pygmy goats and transported them in the trunk of my car to our house, he was a little surprised at my initiative to keep that promise.

Spending six months in such close quarters with Nathan rubbed off on me. I am much more willing to walk into a situation with little or no preparation in order to experience the thrill of attempting to get myself out of it. However, I will say that no matter how much time I spend with him, I will always require my own toothbrush.

At this point in the book, I should probably jot down a few things to recap our experiences and leave my readers with thought-provoking comparisons between Southeast Asia and the United States. However, I have something much more important to write about. Monkeys.

As a reader, if you remember nothing else, please, remember this:

Things Monkeys Hate

Being waved at
Being taunted with bananas
Being treated like monkeys
Having videos taken of them
Seeing your teeth
Cowards
Fake rocks
Being locked up
Running ticket booths
Mustard
Their own feces
Unattractive women
Children
Disruptions during important presentations

Backpack Like You Mean It

1.5 seconds before someone gets their face ripped off.

www.ingramcontent.com/pod-product-compliance
Lightning Source LLC
Chambersburg PA
CBHW051942290426
44110CB00015B/2081